WARREN JORGENSON

DAISIES & DANDELIONS

An Indictment of Today's Parenting

TATE PUBLISHING & *Enterprises*

The opinions expressed by the author are not necessarily those of Tate Publishing, LLC.

Published by Tate Publishing & Enterprises, LLC
127 E. Trade Center Terrace | Mustang, Oklahoma 73064 USA
1.888.361.9473 | www.tatepublishing.com

Tate Publishing is committed to excellence in the publishing industry. The company reflects the philosophy established by the founders, based on Psalm 68:11,
"The Lord gave the word and great was the company of those who published it."

Published in the United States of America

ISBN: 978-1-61777-583-3
1. Political Science / General
2. Social Science / General
11.06.01

TABLE OF
CONTENTS

INTRODUCTION

As recently as fifty years ago, America was a bold, spirited nation. The world regarded America as a bastion of freedom, democracy, wealth, and strength; a large continent settled by European immigrants, wealthy in natural resources and modestly populated. Its God-fearing citizens were envied because of their remarkably high standard of living. The nation invited immigration and was always ready to help the downtrodden. One could come to America and become all that one wanted to be. An individual was free to rise to the level of his or her ability.

The USA was admired as one of the wonders of the world due largely to the Constitution, with its dedication to fundamental rights of the individual and its belief in God. The diverse group of fifty-six signers of the Declaration had set the stage for a noble experiment, the likes of which the world had never seen.

It was a time of exceptionalism in America when young minds might seize onto something that challenged their imagination, and since there were no restraints to ambition, the next thing one knew, he or she might be recognized as a prodigy or even a genius.

Today there are organizations with legions of sympathizers who actually decry America's exceptionalism. Our own president goes out of his way to apologize for America's excellence. *Social justice* has become a prevailing sentiment. America's detractors even frown upon personal wealth and property as, under their breath, they dare to whisper the words *George Soros* and *socialism*.

Should the founding fathers know what America's detractors had in mind for America, they'd be tossing in their graves. America's positive spirit is being usurped by evil and a trend toward socialism.

Democracy, the Constitution, and the American way of life are under a full-frontal attack. America has evolved as the last great hope of the world for all that's good in life. The United States has become the site of a struggle between good and evil. The real battle is between radical liberals and principled conservatives for the hearts, minds and souls of American society.

Should conservative society not receive the kind of voter support necessary to be able to respond to the dangers fostered by the left, in light of the effect it's already having on the nation's wealth and character, America is flirting with the specter of an eventual future as a "banana republic," or worse, a nation in a destitute world controlled by mindless men with guns and knives.

To draw from an analogy, one can have a good lawn and garden until parasites show up, and then before one can turn around, there will be more dandelions than daisies. The analogy is intended to introduce the reader to the thrust of this premise: two different kinds of human nature. Radical progressives, Democrats, liberals, communists, secularists, socialists, etc., are beset with character flaws incurred from early childhood and are dandelions. Principled conservatives, tea baggers, independents, blue-dog Democrats, Republicans, etc., acquired principles and character in early childhood and are daisies. A reader will learn that *what determines one or the other is a matter of parenting*. This premise will indict perhaps as many as half of today's parents as inept, even uncaring.

The fact that there are significant differences between the two kinds of human characteristics and the danger which that poses will be thoroughly addressed. The writer cautions that there are many mental health issues throughout American society far more serious than those touched on here, but undoubtedly they stem from the same root cause.

America's population has grown by half as many people as at the end of World War II and based on the seriousness of conditions in society today most of the population gain had to have been left-leaning liberals and secularists. The conservatives, right leaning, lost their edge a while back, so the nation has been in a state of stress for some time. Sadly with liberals in the ascendancy the gilt-edged magic attached to the term "the American people" is at a point of relative insignificance. Its *prestige* has become almost worthless. The left-leaning Americans—U.S. Congress, the White House administration, the media, the unions and even the stock market *show contempt* for the expression "the American People." The American people have even been relegated by some to the status of "the little people."

There are stars glowing in America's crown again though, and among them are a great number of patriots associating themselves with the tea partiers. The Tea Party Movement, which I hope remains a movement rather than a political party, is *growing*, and it puts fear into the hearts of the left-leaning heavyweights just mentioned. The principled conservatives, the tea partiers, and always the nation's children are America's best prospects for ending the reign of the troubled liberals in the days ahead. They will be fighting an uphill battle from an obvious underdog role.

The *silent-majority* of years ago, the white descendants of the Anglo-Saxon immigrants who pioneered the country, has seen most of its faction return to the earth as dust, but those of us who were of that faction still living should hang our head in shame for allowing religion and the Ten Commandments to be removed from the public schools and for being *silent far too long*. We see what being too complacent on national matters can do to a country. It's imperative that conservative Americans push back on the current administration and the irresponsible loudmouth liberals who are doing America grave harm.

I can't say enough good things about the well-known personalities like Glenn Beck on cable television; Rush Limbaugh on radio; Sarah Palin from her ex-governorship platform; Michelle Malkin, whose biting rhetoric and in-depth research exposes dishonesty; Michele Bachman, the gutsy Republican representative from Minnesota; Ann Coulter, the strong, outspoken journalist; and what others are doing today, i.e., warning the people of increasingly imminent danger. (In case the reader didn't notice, four of the aforementioned "freedom fighters" are female.)

Besides the above, a gentleman deserving of mention here is Jesse L. Peterson, African American president and founder of Brotherhood Organization of a New Destiny (Bond) in Los Angeles, whose consuming passion is rescuing underprivileged youth from the streets of L.A. Reverend Peterson is a courageous, nononsense pastor and conservative with exceptionally broad insight whose voice deserves to be heard across the land. The members of Congress (particularly the black caucus) and the administration should be compelled to hear his message. The writer admires him intensely.

A reminder: my premise broaches the theorem that the earth's population, irrespective of gender or ethnicity, consists of simply two types of people: liberals (dandelions) and conservatives (daisies) and degrees thereof.

I advance the proposition that each person's character meets the criteria intrinsic to one or the other of the above two classifications as a direct consequence of the individual's first five years of life.

I arrived at this premise as a result of studying and cataloging a variety of personal behavior and conduct among children, young people, cohorts, business customers, people in crowds, cable television stories, newspaper stories, articles in periodicals, and the idiosyncrasies of people in general. My interest was doubtless whetted by the two semesters of psychology I had in college. I am confident that this premise holds water, so have chosen to push ahead and offer it up to the public, particularly for its timeliness.

The reader will encounter the terms *liberal*, *progressive*, and *leftist*, which are not political parties as such, but *left-leaning* ideologies identified with the Democrat Party. Conservative, independent, tea party and blue-dog democrats are *right-leaning* ideologies identified with the Republican Party.

A DAISY IN
THE WORKS

I was born in 1921 in a small railroading village in eastern Iowa. My father was the senior of two section foremen living in Bertram, maintaining the Chicago & North Western Railway's high-speed double-track rail system connecting the Union Pacific terminal in Omaha with Chicago and cities in the eastern states.

Because of his safety record, my father was asked to assume the task of maintaining an especially challenging stretch of rail east of the village of Bertram and, after accepting, moved there with my mother and three sisters, two years before I was born. Bertram's population was seventy, mostly railroad families. It was favored with a general store, a church, a two-room elementary school, a community hall, a stockyard and, of course, a depot.

This was at a time of swift, deluxe, transcontinental-passenger trains, and the Union Pacific had more than its share of them, including the renowned Overland Limited, all of which sped through our small village eastward and westward, night after night. The railroad scheduled the Chicago-bound trains to arrive in the "windy city" in the morning hours and leave for the west coast cities around dinnertime. The net effect was that all of the deluxe passenger trains, whether going east or west, crossed Iowa in darkness.

My mother was forty when I was born, the youngest of my sisters being almost eleven years older than me. Occasionally I might overhear my mother offhandedly mentioning to visitors that her son was a "late surprise," and they would chuckle. However, I never noticed any regret on the part of anyone in the family at my late arrival. I'm sure that my mother must have had some apprehension, though, as to how she was going to raise a boy at that late date, especially after having had three girls. My dad was especially glad I came along because I was his first son.

The home had a bedroom downstairs and two upstairs. My two oldest sisters got the one upstairs room with a grate next to the warm chimney that ran up through their room, which was great to stand on before getting into a cold bed for the night. My youngest sister had to share the other smaller, colder upstairs bedroom with me, but Mom gave us the feather mattress as compensation.

Dad was always up first in the morning, building a wood fire in the cook stove in the kitchen on which to heat cold water pumped from the well out on the back porch. The water that Mom drew for the girls to wash with when they came downstairs would be warm by the time the first girl came down to the kitchen. I was always the last one up and sometimes taxed my mother's patience for being too languorous.

We took our meals *together* at a substantial circular oaken table, and eating never began before Mom spoke grace for what we were about to receive. At breakfast time she would serve the meal, never setting herself down to eat until after packing my father's lunch pail and sending him off to work, then us kids to school; then she would sit to have her meal.

My mother was very strict. Her home was indeed her castle and woe it was to anyone who was careless inside the house. For example: we siblings had to clean the soles of our shoes before entering; there was no running inside, no fingerprints on the glass windows or doors; we were to respect the furniture, pick up after ourselves, straighten the bed, wash our hands before meals; there was no slurping when eating soup or cereal; we weren't to be noisy; and there was plentiful use of "please" and "thank you", etc. My pet cat had a comfortable box out in the garage in which to sleep. There would be no pet hair or fur in the house. We did, however, have an American Warbler canary in a cage in the kitchen.

One of Mom's most repeated lectures to us siblings: "We're going to act like civilized human beings in this house, not savages."

Once the family was out of the house in the morning and the dishes and chores were done, Mom always had a task scheduled. The home was spotless, and Mom had an absolute disdain for any woman who wasn't a good homemaker. In addition to her full schedule at home, she was also the treasurer as well as janitor for the church.

Mom was the money manager at home and very frugal. We bought our bread and bakery at a "day-old" store, and in the winter Dad would buy a side of pork or beef from an area-farmer early in the season and saw it into manageable pieces. Mom and the girls would then cold pack most of it with our homegrown vegetables and store the jars in the cellar to see us through the winter. The Mulligan stew was delicious and nutritious.

We didn't own a car until 1935 our travel back and forth to the city of Cedar Rapids, ten miles to the west, being by way of a local train. Dad's employment provided a *pass* that permitted anyone in the family to travel for free on any train on the railroad other than in first-class accommodations. All in all, ours was a happy, spirited family unit.

From as far back as I can remember, I must have been a handful because I remember being swatted on the rump with a ruler or a switch from the lilac bush in the front yard many, many times as I was growing up but Mom *never touched me with her hand*; it was always with some object like a yardstick or a switch from a bush. For her to have used her hand on me would have made the punishment *too personal*, and she would never have been guilty of that. Switching was *simply an admonishment administered immediately after she became aware of the misbehavior*, and the only thing ever injured was my pride. There were no hard feelings afterward.

Mom showed her *love* for me in *many ways*. Hers was not a mushy kind of *love* with a lot of hugs and kisses. She did hug me frequently, but she went out of her way to favor me with things like special treats, pleasant surprises, letting me lick the pastry pans, acquiescing to my special requests, or by caring for me when I needed it. Twice, because my grades were good, she had me excused from school so I could travel with her to California, at a burdensome expense, to see her mother.

She kept the family a cohesive unit and did it in a constant, *loving* way. She was always there for us siblings. She was a tough taskmaster and later on during the three-plus World War II years when I was a prisoner of war of the Japanese, I had ample time to reflect on how her *love and discipline* had strengthened my character while growing up, ultimately saving my life. The love and discipline I experienced in my first five years of life certainly qualified me to be a "daisy" and my mom a "daisy shaper." I remain forever grateful to her memory.

THE ROAD TO AMERICA'S DECLINE

The nation reached its zenith in August 1945 with its victory over the Japanese and the axis powers ending World War II, which the United States won almost single-handedly. After the attack on Pearl Harbor, an enraged American public turned into a country that had never before been concerned about invasion itself and within three and a half years became the greatest military power on earth.

The decline of America began a few years after World War II ended. I lay some of that to revulsion following the use of the A-bombs on Hiroshima and Nagasaki to end the war, which, of course, was brought on by the Japanese themselves with their sneak attack on Pearl Harbor followed by its diabolic display of man's inhumanity to man during the death march on Bataan.

Following the Hiroshima and Nagasaki bombings, logical minds tempered their emotions with the realization that even more and worse revulsion might have to follow in order for the war to end. As it turned out, Japan surrendered, and millions of lives were spared; my life happening to be one of them. With time there would be new families and babies born to both sides. The generations would grow and memories would dim.

The road to ruin, which America seems to be on, began after World War II ended. The nation's victory may very well have been temporary, it winding up a loser in the long run along with every other nation in the world as three potentially harmful circumstances came about at that time.

1. Intoxicated with joy after its overwhelming victory ending World War II, a giddy nation composed of veterans returning home, as well as an American public that had been just as involved in the war effort as they, engaged in adjusting to peace. A general public which had "done without" for almost four years, as well as veterans of both genders anxious to marry and settle down and raise a family, went on an orgy of buying. Everyone was motivated by the notion of owning a *home*. The older folks who had been at home supporting the war effort were of a mind to get back to maintaining and improving theirs while the newly married veterans wanted new ones. *Contrary to the tradition always practiced before the war, i.e., buying only what one could afford, buying was done on the installment plan, and the practice has never ended.*

2. Every American home has a driveway and a garage. Since there were no new cars made during the war, everybody now wanted a new automobile *and often more than one* along with bigger garages. Unlike the "chicken in every pot," the "car in every driveway" was no spoof. The *monstrous consequence of no planning* about how to handle this phenomenon was that almost every individual in America felt the need to own at least one car. As a result, *America's major cities are now basically paralyzed by traffic twice a day for several hours at a time, five days a week,* not to mention the deleterious effects of the huge amount of foul air created. In addition, the nation's super-highways, originally designed for cars, do not anywhere near accommodate the additional huge influx of eighteen-wheelers.

3. A post-World War II entertainment-starved population welcomed the *electronic revolution's* first major entry: *the television set.* Coming to fruition after debuting in 1939, the home entertainment center swept the country by storm with its seductive, siren-like appeal. Its around-the-clock attraction soon usurped the traditional father-mother role in the American home, and it became the personification of role-model in homes all across the country.

Television served a marvelous purpose at first as an entertainment medium, assuring itself permanency in the furniture alignment of practically every living room in America but gradually metastasizing into a cancer eating at the heart of American culture and the human-spirit. In the course of reading Sarah Palin's book, *Rogue*, I was impressed with how her father had handled the television dilemma. He built a shed out in back of the house with a loft where he placed the set. It was unheated, so the kids would have to go outside to the cold shed if they wanted to see something on television. Needless to say, it was only significant programming that they watched.

Traditional conservative practices that had been very popular began becoming much less popular. Exercising, reading and writing, outdoor and indoor game-playing, the family together at the table eating and praying, going to church (religion on the whole suffered), families visiting other families, family-wide picnic events, hobbies, music lessons, trips to the public library, boys tinkering with cars and girls playing with dolls are all examples of how families used to spend time together. Losing ground was principled conservatism; gaining ground was liberalism.

With the passing years went passing school grades. More and more school homework was being sidetracked by this-and-that on television and soon, the nation's report cards were showing the results of learning time wasted. Television didn't go away but eventually its quality did, as well as that of the nation's young brains. I wonder how many of today's parents still have the chutzpah to assign chores to their children.

Education bit the dust as schools boards around the country threw up their hands, giving non-achievers attendance certificates instead of diplomas. Non-achievers, unable to pass the now even lower standards, had to be moved on out of school to make room for those coming along behind. As a consequence, the bell-curve lost its integrity and grade averages flattened out. American society was drifting rapidly into a puddle of mediocrity that has not improved with time. Even universities have suffered; their tenured leftist intellectuals cause many, if not most, to become citadels of liberal ideology rather than education.

Theoretically, at an estimated rate of two hours a day or ten hours-per-week lost to television watching and reduced studying, multiplied by thirty-six school weeks, not to mention time wasted on weekends, the "television generation" had, on average, *at least* 360 fewer hours of learning per school year than seniors of the post-World War II generation. To that, tack on fifty years of lesser education since that time, and one can get a rough, but all-too-generous idea of how a lot of today's lack of learning came about. (Somebody else said it: "When the television set is turned on, all of the air is sucked out of the room.")

With tongue-in-cheek, a cohort has suggested that America has at hand a much better technique for eliciting information from captured terrorists than by waterboarding. He suggests putting manacled terrorists, one at a time, in a windowless room *with a televi-*

sion set turned-on and tuned-in to *a cable news station*; the incessant repetition of the wretched commercials should cause him to begin "singing" within hours, and the media would be demoralized.

Through the years an avalanche of life-easing electronic gadgetry was brought to the market, including the PC (which I see as a good thing). As of this moment, the nation's children and most of its adults deem it essential to stay in touch with each other twenty-four-seven, drowning in technology-overload.

I see nothing good coming of this fascination with communication novelties. There are fewer books being read or written, fewer songs being sung, played, or composed, less physical exercise, fewer pictures being painted, fewer vocabularies being expanded, few lives being transformed, less inspiration being experienced, and the constitution is getting moldy. Time's a-wasting and all the while minds are being absolutely wasted. The individual, the nation, and society will eventually pay a terrible price unless this mindless insanity is stopped. It's a sad commentary on society when a senseless television-creation like "The Simpsons" can command such popularity.

Handwritten English is becoming an almost unacceptable method of communication as texting gains in popularity and there's been a significant dip in common knowledge. It's as if there were an accord discouraging the drudgery of studying to learn; after all, one can Google one's way through life, right? I am told that there are adults who don't even know how to construct or end a sentence or a paragraph.

There is an idiotic word-abbreviating phenomenon sweeping the country, "acronymania," (for want of a better word) and for which there is no glossary to help one decipher them. Electronic devices have become more readily available to enemies of the state, allowing them to be turned against the citizens of the very nation that creates them.

In the ensuing fifty years or so, the once nimble minds of millions of aging citizens of the post-World War II's "great generation" have quite naturally atrophied, putting the seniors at a serious disadvantage with the youth of the nation in terms of today's sophisticated means of communication. To the senior citizen, something as simple as phoning a company or a governmental agency, for example, has become a mind-numbing hassle as the once human voice at the other end has been replaced by an electronic one. With more people aging and more electronic gadgets coming, where does that put the seniors? "Learn to use 'em or lose 'em" it looks like.

With the trend to make life easier and simpler has come sloth. Ambition was throttled as the desire to achieve withered away to make room for more easy living. Among the growing desires of life came labor's plea for job security, and unionism was born. The employer who provided employment and wealth for his employees would now, for example, be told he could not lay-off or discharge an individual that deserved the action. Further, a union-organized strike called on-account of the wages he paid them could bring the employer's business to a costly halt.

Along with the onslaught of liberalism and radicalism came the characteristic of self-love. Narcissism spawned a way of life in which the left-leaning individual waived the virtue of patience for immediate gratification. "One must have it now" has become a prevailing sentiment. It gives lasting credence to the fable of the grasshopper and the ants.

Television has muted the voice of the people for over fifty years now, and when one adds to that the fact that there aren't but a few daily newspapers that one can depend on, the only way the American people get to be heard anymore is by way of polling or at the ballot box. In my opinion, television and electronic novelties continue to be *the most insidious, destructive forces* in the nation today.

RHYTHM AND ORDER

Long before a smidgeon of civilization sprang from the countless tribes populating earth, there were aged wise men observing that life on the planet had a rhythm to it. Day followed night; fair weather followed foul; ocean waves had a rhythm; season followed season, to which flora and fauna of the earth reacted rhythmically; birds and animals migrated within a pattern; the moon, the constellations, and the stars had rhythmic cycles, etc., and with realization came certainty.

Tribes that were nomadic could cease being on the move, choosing promising land on which to settle, the land looking like they could grow crops there. A whole new kind of culture would be born. As time moved forward, so also did learning and intelligence. With that intelligence came the knowledge that life on earth was not intended to be complex, but *that it must have order and harmony*. Mankind learned that it needed food, shelter, clothing, water, and time for rest. It also learned that the tribe must reproduce to sustain itself. Its members must be industrious and always plan for a tomorrow.

Recorded history, beginning with the most archaic of methods, has been the guiding light for successive generations down through the ages. One of the most important things learned from history was that the great leaders depended upon their aged wise men for guidance. Their *wisdom*, acquired from years of experience, made it expedient that the leaders draw on them for advice, and they did so constantly. They comprised a leader's cabinet, so to speak.

I'm sure that those wise men, if they could speak to us, would admonish us not to tinker with human nature or anything of God's doing; a most appropriate consideration today as radical liberal elements continue to try overriding strong, conservative aversion to casual sex, unnatural sex, and untraditional marriage.

The sources of *genuine wisdom* in any country *are the elder* statesmen. This is as true today as it was hundreds and thousands of years ago. Today's waste of the wisdom-of-senior's is at a time when youth's hysterical chant for "change" is making for serious problems. These are the folks who should be sitting on *city councils* instead of foolishly handing off the positions to young students attending college, which is common in many municipalities.

Older folks may not be "pretty people", there being so many who don't take care of their bodies like they should. The best, most productive years of one's life, however, are from about age sixty to seventy-five, plus-a-few years perhaps, when one has finally accrued wisdom. Far too many are admittedly obese and sloppy, not to mention infirm and dull, so it's easy to see why the leftist ilk might be indifferent toward seniors. On balance, though, the aged conservative population certainly has a lot more wisdom to offer the nation than *the youth culture* that doesn't even know the meaning of decorum.

Years ago there was a body of elder statesmen of mixed gender retired from the movie industry who were organized to help give it positive direction (I hesitate to use the term "police it," as it was powerless) called the Hayes office. The industry didn't like being subjected to constant scrutiny by the body, but on the whole, it benefited greatly from the *principled* guiding influence.

With as many well-qualified, older individuals among American society as there are today, *all industries and even the nation's Congress* would do well to have some *freelance* body of principled retirees acting in the capacity of counsel. Such a practice would be valuable, lending an always-needed principled guidance. It would be particularly valuable at this time of financial stress and even for the future. I'm sure consumers would welcome the step enthusiastically.

Through the years, earth's cycles retained their rhythm, but the people tenanting it surely did not. America strayed from the traditional rhythm and order that made it great late in the 1950's. Then in the sixties, conditions degenerated almost into anarchy as huge segments of the post-war generation turned their collective back on the *family*-structure and rebelled. The nation's society should have seen the writing on the wall then for what it was, and done something about it. This was the first significant evidence of *permissive parenting* where there was an absolute absence of parental authority.

In the sixties, in a fit of degeneracy, large numbers of undisciplined, empty-headed youth hit the road aimlessly, large numbers winding up living on the streets, many ejaculating their indecency at Woodstock. The Supreme Court removed religion from the schools, and the Vietnam War was taken to new heights, only to have a policy turnabout in Washington defame the cause for which thousands of cream of American youth had given their lives. In the same breath, it made a gift of the country they had been defending to the terrorists, thereby opening the door for the Pathet Lao to slaughter hundreds of thousands of Vietnamese who'd been loyal to the USA. There were race riots in the South; President Kennedy was assassinated, then his brother, and then Martin Luther King, Jr. as well.

Circumstances have steadily deteriorated; the mammoth growth of the liberal culture in recent generations has been at the expense of conservatism. Television has continued to be the role model in American homes at the expense of *parenting*. The safety of the nation is in the balance; the liberal issue has passed from one of toleration to *cause for major concern.*

It's regrettable that eyes of the jaundiced liberals are absolutely blind to something as important as quality in a person. Obviously it's because they don't have any themselves, inner quality that is.

The nation is going to need a whole new rebirth under God, and the good Lord willing, should there be a government emerging led by conservatives, it will undoubtedly recognize and reaccept into the mainstream the mature, experienced minds that the democrats have been wasting. I pray that this shall come to pass.

THE PRINCIPLED
CONSERVATIVE

As defined by Webster, a *principle* is a fundamental truth or proposition that serves as the foundation for a system of belief or behavior or for a chain of reasoning, for example, the basic *principles* of Christianity.

The American Constitution incorporated Christian principles that the citizens were proud to live by and which stood them in good stead for more than two hundred years. Those principles, of biblical origin, contributed significantly to setting American society apart, head and shoulders above other world governments. The large majority of those Americans and their descendants have been pleased to call themselves conservatives and, from inception, have embraced tradition and Christianity.

Conservative individuals truly love America with all of its warts and blemishes and are outspoken about that love. They are unabashedly pleased and proud of the nation and its constitution. They will rally round the flag at a moment's notice. They are characteristically constrained by principles of decency and fairness in the way they talk and act, so dialogue is measured, low-key, and free of stridence, devoid of untruth, and generally has a point to it. They are for small government. The older folks are all that remain of the Yankee Doodle Dandies, the descendants of the Anglo-Saxon immigrant pioneers, and to me, *all* are desirable, patriotic, enthusiastic Americans; *they are the daisies.*

What determines whether an *infant* will become a "dandelion" or a "daisy"? *Parenting is the answer*, and on the next page, one will learn how to *recognize the difference between the* two. I feel that I can't say enough about *parenting*, so this may be the defining chapter of this premise. *I firmly believe that* all *new parents should receive detailed instruction in child rearing, as far too many are abdicating their responsibilities. A textbook of knowledge about child rearing* and the part *principles should play* in *parenting* is dearly needed and urged to be required reading. Within such a book, there should be at least one full chapter devoted to *young females* especially, recognizing them as unique human beings that should receive *special education* as to the nature of their womanhood.

New parents should be made aware that the time is coming when parents will be *required to be responsible for their children*. In today's dangerous world, that kind of legislation has become imperative, privacy arguments to the contrary.

Normally, a lot should happen in a home before a child is enrolled in school. To have a healthy child at five, those first five years must incorporate a lot of preparation. During the first two years particularly, the child needs a proper diet, rest, exercise, and *discipline*. The child must learn personal hygiene and, *most importantly, be given lots of love.*

Seldom, if ever, discussed openly is the subject of whether or not one's offspring was conceived in an atmosphere of love or in lust, but it matters. A man and wife take pride in reflecting that their child was conceived in an atmosphere of love. A child conceived during the coupling of a mutually dedicated man and wife, barring unforeseen circumstances, is generally going to become a positive, warm, outgoing human being, the mark of a conservative.

Parents who conceive a child in an attitude of love are secure in the knowledge that *if* a child should come of the union, it will be *legitimate* and *welcome* in a family structure and, above all, *loved. It is absolutely essential, particularly during the period from infancy to five, that the child feels welcome at all times.*

Infants are not born principled. A young child is much like an unbroken horse. The animal can be physically healthy, able to eat, sleep, walk, etc., but cannot be ridden and enjoyed, made worthwhile, until broken to bridle and bit; only then does it become whole/rideable. A term perhaps more appropriate to human beings is the word *humbled*. (The word *humble* can have a negative connotation, but the thrust of its meaning is deference to authority.)

Children who are products of a regimen of love and discipline, humbled as it were, develop into happy and contented youth and/or team players that won't usually rebel when reaching their teens. *Any woman who has given birth* probably knows what it feels like to be humbled once she lays eyes on her baby.

Ever since Adam and Eve, we've known that the human being is born with a rebellious nature, which is brought under control via *discipline* at the hands of the parent. By way of a mix of discipline and tender affection, starting very young, future conservative *adults* acquire *principles*, which the Bible refers to as fruits of the Spirit: love, *joy, peace, patience, kindness, goodness, faithfulness, gentleness, and self-control.* With possession of these biblical principles comes an inner peace and happiness that only a conservative can enjoy. Additionally, the infant learns how to play, how to imagine, how to communicate and will be receptive to learning about God, prayer, etc. This knowledge has come down through the ages, so it is irrefutable. These positive qualities are not to be found in a loveless environment.

I should point out that the principled conservative's idea of discipline generally is a simple swat on the child's rump, preferably with a ruler or a stick, or something like that, *at the moment of misbehavior.* Not later! *Love* should be shown later.

The temperament acquired by a product of a love-and-discipline environment becomes so imbued upon that individual's nature that it's as indelible and unremitting as an ID card. It is there for life. This holds true for every single individual who ever experienced a prolonged interval of love and discipline as a child. The *positive principles* are as much a mark of true conservatism today as they were fifty or a hundred years ago with the large majority of the American population then. It's my experience that today's liberal harbors only negative ones.

I am mindful of the ridicule, contempt, disdain, etc., that ultra-liberals directed at television series like *The Walton's*, *The Andy Griffith Show*, *Ponderosa*, and *Little House on the Prairie*, etc., because they portrayed life as too saccharin sweet, enough so as to make some want to vomit, it was said. The old-fashioned portrayals, though faithful to traditional conservative American values, were *so morally principled* that far-out liberals just couldn't handle it. *The ultra-liberal revulsion at moral principle remains in vogue yet today.*

There was a large gathering in August of 2010 at the mall in Washington DC. It was made up of several-hundred thousand "tea baggers" who came together to protest tax measures and pool their feelings about freedom and liberty. When the event was over, there was no garbage left to be picked up. The tea party conservatives typically cared for their own trash.

If there ever should come a time or an occasion when *a liberal might try to* act like a *conservative, it* could *never succeed* because he or she wouldn't have the positive moral principles necessary to be *conscientious.* Through the eyes of a liberal, the tea-party conservatives are probably seen as "neat freaks."

With the daisy-dandelion concept being openly discussed, the question arises: how might one distinguish one from the other? There is no measurable test; it's a matter of recognizing either a positive or negative *pattern of behavior*/conduct and/or an equivalent kind of rhetoric.

Behavior and/or rhetoric determine how one is recognized.

A liberal will recognize a *conservative* by way of any of the previously enunciated *nine positive biblical principles*, plus additional positive principles/characteristics shown here:

1. confidence
2. helpfulness
3. grace
4. honesty
5. generosity
6. frugality
7. sincerity
8. courage
9. order
10. realism

11. humility
12. consideration
13. responsibility
14. optimism
15. volunteerism
16. consideration
17. trust
18. respect
19. logic
20. patriotism
21. with humor
22. ambition

Generally speaking, a liberal's behavior will be *opposite the above.*

One should not try to make an association as to which-is-of-which temperament by way of a political party because there are going to be Democrats who are conservative by nature and conversely Republicans who will be *left leaning by nature.* Where there may be doubt, the basic criteria are *who's principled* and *who's not.*

Though the conservative's and liberal's human nature will remain relatively constant, one must concede that there will be some degree of deviation from the precise definition due to some measure of *affection and discipline* experienced by a liberal during childhood, while on the other hand a conservative individual may have experienced a measure of disaffection during childhood without destroying his or her principle(s). *Love and discipline* will remain *constant*s however.

The conservative's characteristics above are not meant to imply that he or she is somehow more "perfect" or "better" than another individual; it's just that he or she had more responsible parenting. The conservative is quite capable of doing silly, foolish, or dumb things. The principled conservative has a good grasp of whom he or she is though; where one is headed in life and, as a consequence, has a good measure of self-assurance. However, for all of the brownie points accredited to principled conservatism, it has a *seriously dangerous downside* to contend with, and that is *complacency*.

The *consequence of complacency* is that conservatives are often mistakenly seen by liberal elements as being weak and become aggressive toward them. The conservative surely has the inner strength to tolerate aggression, but it's been my experience that one's well-being is better served *by being more assertive and to confront such behavior*. Complacency accounts for why the "silent-majority" label was applied to the post-World War II adults who said nothing and kept their feelings under wraps while liberalism and immorality romped roughshod across the moral fabric of American society.

For all the fine things about being a principled conservative, past history shows them to be a bit like the fabled *Rip Van Winkle* who needed to be awakened from his twenty-year sleep from time to time to bring him up-to-date on what'd been going on around him. Much credit, incidentally, is due those principled conservatives who *had the* courage to step forward and become part of the tea party movement.

Hopefully this study may serve as a wake-up call for conservatives to come alive, to be more assertive, to unite with other conservatives, and begin to take steps to take back the nation from a troubled liberal populace. It also is intended as an opportunity for individuals who may be experiencing anxiety or are apprehensive about their liberal lifestyle to become converts-to- Christianity and thereby bring peace and happiness into their life.

Were I to be asked to *point to an example* that might confirm the relevance of the love-and-discipline concept, I would point to the *Amish people*; their general conduct mirrors the kind of philosophy that the principled conservative espouses.

The liberal who might tag conservatives as "holier than thou" may wonder from time to time and ask, what's so different between him or her and a principled conservative? The answer is not a great deal. The *frame of* reference is that life on earth is a constant battle between good and evil, *the same struggle existing within every human being*, liberal or conservative, all the time. There's absolutely no difference between people up to that point. The difference occurs when an individual's parents were *caring and responsible* during the child's infancy and God was made a part of the equation.

The following is not intended to be a lecture, rather *excerpted knowledge from the Bible: God sent Jesus Christ to earth to die for the sins of mankind, thus enabling people* who surrender their lives to Christ *to acquire the power of the Holy Spirit within them, enabling them to pray to God, to talk with him, to be given eternal life, and to shut-out evil from their lives.*

From the beginning of time when Adam and Eve angered God, the consequence was that mankind would forever have to struggle with good (godliness) and evil (Satan) within one's inner being. One must surely acknowledge the presence of gremlins of good and evil struggling within each of us from time-to-time today.

Lest there be any doubt on the part of a reader, America was founded to escape oppressive English law that interfered with the freedom to worship God in churches of their choice. Almost all of the signers of the Declaration were devoutly religious men. So from the birth of America, praying to God has been as important as life itself for the founders and, by association, the American people. Our ancestors were godly and conservative, so the principles exemplified in the Scriptures became part of the tapestry of American history, as did the tradition of love and discipline in the family. Those elements are in-bred into the principled conservative person's nature.

The growth of the *dissident leftist* element exploded after World War II with the advent of television when the hypnotic nature of the machine destroyed the family unit and brought about a shift by the young *from* family-and-tradition toward "progress" and "change." With it went godliness and morality, and the schism between liberalism and conservatism continued to grow. For the last fifty years or so, America has been *blanketed by a cloud of radical liberalism* that has "shut out the sun."

Beneath the cloud, a God-endowed land is still intact. It has had to contend with overwhelming evil for a long time, but remains at heart a Christian nation. It allowed itself to be spirited away from its high road by evil liberal elements in the Democratic Party and too much complacency on the part of conservatives, but the spirit is thriving again and appears to be reasserting itself.

Fortunately today's conservative family still resembles the traditional family as it has come down through the years, living life the American way. It sits at the table together, eats together, loves together, talks together, plays together, cries together, and prays together. The down-to-earth conservative family sets the standard by which all other families should be measured.

It should be pointed out, that up until the time of President Clinton's impeachment by the House of Representatives in 1998, the Republican Party was the *conservative political party, standing for all the* positive principles *that had been its hallmark down through the years. Then that august Republican body,* which actually held the majority at the time, *strangely,* sold out its values *to the Democratic* minority *in the Senate, which defied protocol, and* refused to follow constitutional procedure *in the impeachment of*

President Clinton who was guilty of grossly immoral acts. (It's my sense that it was that dangerous complacent nature of the conservative *that led to the Republicans' downfall.)*

One can never forget, Senator Joe Biden with *Republican Majority Leader,* Senator Trent Lott and Rick Santorum at his side, telling Representative Henry Hyde, who had *succeeded* in voting a bill of impeachment of President Clinton through the House of Representatives, *that in the Senate "they did things their way"* (forget constitutional procedures), the Senate body then regrettably voting to exonerate him.

The fact that the person occupying the highest office in the American government could be party to sleazy sexual indiscretions with a young female intern while in office and be tried on the world stage before television cameras and not be impeached dismayed American conservatives and people around the world. To their everlasting shame, the Republicans in the senate were seen as cowardly for surrendering to the Democrat minority, whose most strident voices were Senators Kennedy, Biden, Dodd, Schumer, Durbin, Boxer, Harkin, Leahy and the late Sen. Byrd and things in Washington have not been the same since. *The Democrats* poisoned the well when they refused to follow constitutional protocol in the Senate, *all drinking from the same cup, including the Republicans.*

For little-known shocking, damning knowledge about the Democratic Party and the U.S. Senate during this shameful page in history, *one should read the book* Sell Out, *still available online at www.regnery.com by David*

Schippers, who was Chief Investigative Counsel for the Clinton impeachment.

Ever since Bill Clinton's indecency, the Democratic Party has been one of evil deception, corruption, and mischievous intrigue. Names among the Clinton legal defense community of less-than-noble quality like John Podesta and David Boies are still very much part of the party's deplorable nature. For example: today John Podesta is CEO of the Center for American Progress, a leftist-front organization.

President Bush's *new* administration had the dubious pleasure of working with the morally damaged goods who survived the 2000 election. Truth be known, there were a lot of *guilty consciences* roaming the halls of Congress after Clinton's impropriety and, *shamefully, many of them are still there*. The consequences of Bill Clinton's immoral acts while occupying the highest office in the land are still rippling through Congress, despite desperate Democratic attempts to launder away the evil scent.

The long-range consequences to Bill Clinton's perversity have undoubtedly contributed more than somewhat to America's steep descent into immorality. The fact that he has maintained or perhaps even enhanced his status in society doesn't help to dissipate the shadow of evil lingering over Washington and society, all the more reason that *stand-up principled conservatism* is needed desperately to reverse America's leftist direction.

THE LOVELORN
LEFTIST

This chapter confronts the abnormal evil spirit of liberalism and the radical left. For openers, a reader should be reminded that liberals have an adversarial attitude toward conservatism because of revulsion toward *goodness* and things positive. The primary left-leaning entities are the democrats and liberals, but to those groups should be added the body of Progressives. In the politically correct world of today, the term *progressive* has a positive connotation when, in truth, it is anything but. Thanks to David Horowitz's booklet, "Barack Obama's Rules for Revolution," we learn that in the 1940s, Communists played a role in the creation of the CIO, a "progressive" coalition of industrial unions led first by John L. Lewis and then by Walter Reuther, who was a socialist. (David Horowitz has also published another booklet of sixteen pages entitled "The Art of Political War for Tea Parties," which is a must read.)

Since the term *progressive* has left-leaning credence and there is even a Progressive-caucus active in Washington, *left-leaning entities will be consolidated here as liberals*, collectively meeting the criteria for the term "dandelions."

Collectively, the liberals' numbers may approximate the conservative population, so their influence on politics and social behavior make them a force, though not a unified one, to be reckoned with. Collectively, the liberal's inherent malodorous behavior and the conservative's indifference toward it after World War II contributed to the nation's descent into the moral abyss where America finds itself today.

What defines a liberal? His or her albatross is a character flaw occurring during the period of infancy to age five, when the parents will have either short-changed the infant of normal/traditional love and discipline or indicated to the child, if only for a moment or two that it was not wanted. An infant dare not sense such a dangerous lapse of its security on the part of its parents. Merely *lacking in a sufficiency of love and discipline, the psyche becomes indelibly flawed—flawed how much depends upon the measure of love and discipline that may or may not have been experienced by the infant in those early days. Anyway, there is an inner longing for approval, an emptiness, so* the liberal is a troubled person. *Such a person's temperament evolves to a different mind-set than that of a principled conservative.*

If one should ever lose sight of the fact that liberals are not like conservatives, unprincipled *people, as opposed to* principled, *turn to conservative Michelle Malkin's book* Unhinged, *in which she captures the essence of the true offensive liberal. It could be a textbook on "How to Release Inner Torment." In it are two-hundred some pages (a journal, as it were) of verifiable, revolting nastiness and filth issuing from the sick minds of distressed liberals, most of it excerpted from the Internet, striking out at her as a result of her previous book critical of the Democrats.*

To a principled conservative, that kind of thought process strikes alarm because it's so loathsome, so revolting, so far out of character from what one might expect to issue from a supposedly normal mind. It's difficult for the conservative mind to grasp the fact that another human being's mind could be so full of hate and negativity in its criticism of one, let alone that it's just because his or her professionalism is offensive to them. It goes to show what conservatism is up against in day-to-day contact with the liberal left.

If one were to line up a hundred people and then walk down the line and try to pick out liberals from conservatives, one couldn't do it. Only by observing another's *behavior* can one make the distinction. This is oversimplified, but for example, if one is quick to anger, that person is a liberal. One who is helpful and considerate is a conservative. A person who is impolite or indifferent to another person is a liberal. One who is soft-spoken or polite is a conservative, etc.

It's certain that many individuals whom I classify as liberals in this premise are radical revolutionaries who have far more serious mental disorders than a troubled mind. One end of the liberal spectrum *is* more violent than the other. There is no doubt, and crime statistics bear me out, that there are huge numbers of left-leaners in society who are actually dangerous psychopaths but sufficiently competent to hold a job. Simple observation may acknowledge behavior patterns in an individual, but barring marked misbehavior, there is not much one can do about it.

Circumstances on the Hill suggest that there may be a number of them in Washington. National safety and security dictate that a method be found that can set these potentially dangerous individuals apart from normal society, some needing actual confinement.

A liberal has a decided tendency to blame other people or circumstances for his or her own inadequacies and is characteristically negative, quick to anger, pushy, unapologetic, unprincipled, impolite, arrogant, selfish, dissatisfied, immature, irresponsible, restless, stubborn, hateful, deceitful, vindictive, offensive, vicious tempered, devoid of conscience, and contemptuous of Christianity—*characteristics in* direct opposition *to those of the conservative. A liberal is in constant need of a scapegoat to ridicule, to reinforce one's lack of security. Though a liberal may disagree with adjudged characterizations, in the final analysis actual visible behavior will always be the arbiter. (By one's actions and rhetoric, will one be known.)*

Raising a child is serious business, and the first five years of a child's life can be like a jungle if it has to grow up in an environment where the parents are not in love, are indifferent, are quarrelsome, are mean to the child, or where maybe one parent has walked out and there's just a stressed single parent present. In the "good old days" (fifty or so years ago), these kinds of conditions would be out of the norm, but today they may very well be the norm, considering how much emotional strife there is.

Whether it's in a home having just a single parent or one consisting of a male and female (married or unmarried) or a pregnancy outside of marriage but with no genuine enduring love or affection present, a child is very likely to be subjected to damaging negative elements. Chances are that one of the parents, or both, might regard the pregnancy as having been an "accident" or even a "trap" and will raise the child indifferently or, in some cases, even wishing it hadn't been born.

I'm convinced that it's at the hands of impatient, deceptive, short-tempered parents that huge numbers of unreported child-abuse incidents resulting in mental as well as physical crippling abnormalities originate. The privacy phenomena really ties authority's hands here.

Negative characteristics are no respecters of people, descending on single parents, loveless couples, or relationships alike. Pregnancies in single females are not likely to have been conceived in an attitude of love but more likely in a coupling of lust, even though a degree of affection could have been present at the moment. It's possible that such a single mother, rejected by a promiscuous male, might conceivably care enough to bestow a measure of her own genuine love and discipline on a new baby and raise it alone, thereby saving it from falling victim to dysfunction. It's always better, of course, for a father figure to be present.

President Barack Obama is a victim of a broken home, his father having run away from Barack's white mother and parental responsibility to return to Kenya. Barack was then raised by his white grandparents.

I think that in some liberal residences, the family dog gets more affection and discipline than a child. Dogs' minds are good enough for learning to obey, for learning tricks, and to recognize who provides their biscuits, but beyond that they're not very complex. On the other hand, the child that springs from one's own loins is a fantastically *complex* bundle of protoplasm with huge potential from age one to high school and deserves the fullest measure of attention right from birth.

In a broken home or relationship or any negative, loveless environment, a child is going to experience rejection, rebuke, resentment, angst, indifference, dislike, distrust, frustration, helplessness, loneliness, fear, indecision, etc.— all toxic characteristics that will "come home to roost" sooner or later and manifest themselves in anger at society. The unhappier the childhood, the more vitriolic the hatred a leftist will harbor. *This is certainly the breeding ground for crime.* Crime does not originate in homes of responsible parents. *Particularly worrisome is the fact that the number of disturbed youth today who tend to be suicidal is up by myriad numbers.*

In any case, it's into loveless/lustful environments that millions of liberals continue to be born and raised, certainly not desirable places into which an infant should start life.

Consider the women whose marriages break up due to desertion, divorce, rape, incest, etc., and it's mind-boggling to realize what a terribly serious problem America has with huge numbers of bastardized children. They're outside of the mainstream of normalcy, so without special attention, they are going to grow up to become aberrant liberal adults.

Liberals are consumed with a desire for change. They have wrapped themselves in the term *progress* and deluded themselves into thinking that it's some kind of magic phenomena for going forward. Liberals are troubled with America's history and its shortcomings. They tend to blame capitalism for the nation's ills. They demean the military constantly, believing that America is an aggressor nation. It would strike dread into the heart of a liberal if the United States were to stand up for something today fearing some kind of reprisal. They are for big government. They are sympathetic to *globalism* for solving the world's issues.

They feel that the constitution is "old hat," that it is an obstruction, that it is too outspoken about what the government *can't* do *to* the individual and not enough about what it *can* do *for* the individual, therefore has served its purpose and could be dispensed with. Their loyalties to America do not extend beyond lip service. (I'd be curious to know if many young liberals enlist in the military. Perhaps, when one is broke and needs the money.)

Like the secularist's attitude toward religion, the liberal thinks that human beings can manage satisfactorily without strong leadership. They criticize and complain loudly about authority and military force but conveniently look the other way when really abusive social issues to which they're vulnerable are brought up, like the use of drugs, liquor, tobacco, and marijuana.

Liberals feel unconstrained by principles or troubled by consequences, so they feel free to enunciate their feelings loudly, to say anything they want about anyone, about any issue, wherever or whenever they want, whether true or not, as long as it serves their purposes, so they are not trustworthy. In arguments, they generally dwell on points that are irrelevant.

Overwhelming evidence mounts daily that liberals in politics have absolutely no self-control, especially when it comes to spending someone else's money. Consequently, it's desirable that the liberal democrats be kept in the minority in national and state legislatures to avoid their achieving chairmanship and appropriation positions; witness leftist Barney Frank and his exorbitantly expensive illicit-relationship with Fannie Mae and Freddie Mac.

Liberals are of a secular bent, perhaps willing to concede that God created the earth but would insist that he turned it over to human beings to manage. They tend to become furious at any mention of Jesus Christ. The Bible states: "To have everlasting life, one has to come to him through his son—Jesus Christ—who shed his blood on the cross to forgive the sins of mankind." Those words inspire venomous, liberal hatred.

Conservatives would do well to learn the nature of a liberal. They'll be less apt to be hurt by a chance unloved person. A single girl or boy, for example, who has not experienced genuine love and discipline from a parent is a terrible prospect for a marriage partner. The liberal is incapable of bonding. It's *an unalterable fact: one cannot give love if he or she has not received love.*

I cannot stress enough the desperate need for detailed parenting instruction, new school curriculum, and legislation making parents responsible for their children in order to reverse the alarming trend toward dysfunction.

The following is a partial listing of attitudes and behavior patterns typically embraced by members of today's liberal population. A conservative would do well to study them to better acquaint oneself with some of the negative characteristics of dysfunction. These liberal behavior issues fly in the face of an opposite kind of behavior on the part of conservatives:

1.	A preoccupation with sex	10.	An immersion in gadgetry
2.	Irresponsible	11.	A disdainfulness for authority
3.	Indifference toward illegitimacy	12.	Ineptness at raising family
4.	Reluctance to set goals	13.	Absence of self-control
5.	Contempt for Christianity	14.	Porno viewer
6.	Absence of willpower	15.	Often a homosexual
7.	A morbid fascination with food	16.	Unfaithfulness
8.	A carelessness about littering	17.	A Practioner of deceit
9.	Fickleness	18.	Abortion supporter

All of these characteristics are not necessarily going to be present in the character of all liberals. The liberal may disagree with these adjudged behavior patterns, but actual visible behavior will always be the arbiter.

Because of political correctness and public hysteria about privacy, it's not easy to point out or to speak out about many *criminally bent* liberals who are scofflaws and worse. In an aside, it's worth noting that the liberals who indulge in the filth of pornography and mood-altering substances are in remarkable contrast to the decent way in which the principled conservatives live.

As difficult as the subject of the liberal phenomenon is to propound, considering its scope within society, on the whole it will be seen as an illness plaguing society, which will heal with time. Not only will time allow for attrition to take place within the liberal population, but it will permit a new and different emphasis on parenting and positive childhood education to be established. There could also be a wave of revulsion at the nature of liberalism, resulting in a resurgence of Christianity, further hastening American normalcy.

It's fair to point out that those individuals harboring liberal characteristics are not necessarily doomed to carry them for the rest of one's life; one can eliminate them from his or her person at any time by converting to Christianity and one can do that *in one's own domicile by simply getting down on one's knees and praying, imploring God to listen.*

Shortcomings on the part of a parent(s) in a liberal's early upbringing caused him or her to be denied the positive principle of integrity. *Consequently, he or she is just not the traditional, enthusiastic, loyal, patriotic kind of good American citizen. Liberals are the dandelions.*

LOVE

After I graduated from college in 1951, my first employment was as a sales and promotion rep with the independent Capitol Records distributor in Iowa's capital city. Throughout the fifties, Nat King Cole was recording for the Capitol label, and it was a joy to sell and promote his records and albums. (To me and friends of mine in the music business, Nat King Cole was the consummate romantic vocal, jazz, and piano artist of all time. Sinatra wasn't in the same league.)

It's not just coincidence that I'm writing about Nat King Cole and love; it is because one of the most tender, meaningful ballads that Nat Cole ever recorded was the song "Nature Boy." If one has not heard it, one must make every effort to do so before he or she leaves this mortal coil. The lovely closing lyrics of that beautiful song pretty well sum up what life is all about, i.e., "the greatest thing you'll ever learn is to love and be loved in return."

The love that the song "Nature Boy" conjures is so all-encompassing, so tender, so deep, and so meaningful it still causes me to become teary upon hearing. I feel sad when thinking about the many children and adults who have never experienced deep, affectionate love and maybe never will.

Love is the most important element I can introduce into this narrative. It is, perhaps, the most important ingredient in any of our lives. The whole thrust of this narrative is about the difference *between two types of human beings, conservative and liberal, and love or* the lack of it *(as well as some discipline). After mother's milk, love is the single most important thing a mother can give a frightened new human being that's been safe and secure in her womb for those many months. From its first few breaths, the new life's nature is going to be shaped as to whether it'll be a contented conservative or a lovelorn liberal. Without a dedication of genuine love, security, and discipline on the part of parents (or at least one parent) for the couple of years ahead, the child is well on it's way to becoming a disturbed, liberal human being.*

It's mind-boggling to even contemplate the immensity of this issue, how love, or the absence of it, during an individual's infancy can so affect the direction of an individual's life and, in truth, the lives of the whole world's people. On the one hand, it speaks to careless indifference on a massive scale—millions of liberal parents who missed-out on love in their early life, possessing limited or no sense of values. It's depressing to think that liberal couples can be just casually concerned or maybe not concerned at all, about the future of a frightened new child who they themselves spawned, but this is happening every day.

On the other hand, it's also mind-boggling to look at the new child through another set of eyes, those of a principled conservative, and realize how precious that new life is, what a magnificent creation, and to think that it was spawned by two adults who love each other.

Down through the years, it's been normal for young people to confuse physical attraction with love. The interval is very exciting; one feels affection for the other, and the two may feel that they never want to be apart. This "glow" might be the real thing, the beginning of a true enduring love, but then again it might not. Considering what's at stake, i.e., a lifetime of wondrous adventure ahead, plus one's self-respect, a well-founded conservative girl or boy may not want to make a careless mistake at this point in one's life, so he or she might want to abstain from sexual experimentation, at least until he or she conducts one's own test for signs of moral principles within the object of one's affection.

A knowing young lady is aware of her unique state and, if properly mentored, will carry herself with proper pride. She will find herself irresistible, especially to the man of her choice, and she'll be full of confidence as a wife. A girl who loses her virginity prior to marriage, though, loses that delightful, immaculate aura that is so attractive in the bearing of a young woman. Young conservatives would do well to have in mind a test ahead of time that would help them size up another person. An unnoticeable test could help one avoid making a big mistake.

It's reassuring to realize that real, honest-to-goodness love, like what God must have had in mind when he took Adam's rib and made Eve, exists among couples in love yet today. I'm convinced that careful thought must first be given, however, and groundwork laid, for that wonderful relationship to develop. For example, a good marital relationship developing between a liberal and a conservative is next to impossible because of the difference in their basic human natures.

It's been my experience that a marriage built on a strong foundation of love is a marriage made in heaven. Choosing one's lifetime mate is likely the most important thing one will ever do. Down the road, there will hopefully be children, and *then* what life is really all about happens. Sometime later, one becomes blessed further by the love of family and kinfolk.

A pleasant-byproduct of writing is the occasional coming together of scattered thoughts making for a whole new perspective on something that one has been reaching for but unable to put into words. It came to me in a dream. It was of a time when I was a kid, probably around twelve or thirteen. I had a pet cat, named Buff for his color. My mother was a tidy housekeeper and she wasn't going to have any cat fur in her house, so Buff slept out in the garage. He was comfortably in out of the weather and the bed was a cardboard box with an old blanket to lie on. He seemed to enjoy it immensely. On summer afternoons he delighted in sleeping in the sun on a wooden bench alongside the garage. Sometimes when he wasn't sprawled-out but just reposing with his paws folded under him, I'd set down by him and pet him, rubbing the tips of my fingers all about his head and under his chin. He'd close his eyes and soak-up the pleasure and pretty soon he'd start purring – a soft, kind of rattly sound that I enjoyed because I knew he was loving what I was doing.

I got to thinking about that pleasant dream about my pet cat and made-the-leap to how that practice wasn't unlike what a man should do for his "significant other". After all, the female human-being seems to have some of a cat's nature in her. There's nothing new about that; probably most every man has compared a girl or a woman to a cat in some way at sometime or other.

I had never thought about it in this way before, but evidently God intended for Eve to be more than just a companion, but a loving-companion to Adam, to be loved and petted.........not in a sexual way, that's carnal pleasure and there's a place for that, but in a kind, considerate and thoughtful way.

Like the cat who can be made to purr, the human female will purr in her own way in response to petting and love by her male partner, and he'll receive pleasure that can't be measured. I know for a fact, that a fulfilled and appreciated wife will do unpleasant tasks for a husband and never complain. She'll do the housekeeping, the cooking, making the beds, grocery shopping, caring for the needs of the children - sick and well, delivering them and picking them-up from school, doing the family's laundry and ironing etc., etc.

Though it is drudgery, she'll be happy all the while knowing that she's loved by a man who will show his love and appreciation for her. She must be told by him frequently that he loves her. He should show it by way of help around the house, pleasant surprises like going-out to dine or to a show, or with endearing gifts, or trips or just by rubbing her back and her feet........like petting a pussy cat. It'll pay heavenly dividends. It follows that us men should quit being so selfish, always thinking about ourselves, and see our "lady-loves" as the loving companions that they are.

Perhaps the most meaningful definition of love in Webster's Dictionary, among many, is: "a strong affection for another arising out of kinship or personal ties," like for one's offspring, one's kin, one's mate, one's friend, or even for one's country. This definition most squarely supports what I feel are the ultimate manifestations of love, i.e., *tears* of joy, *tears* of patriotism and *tears* of sadness.

Love of country ought to be shared by all of us Americans, but regrettably it's not necessarily shared by the liberal enclave. It's next to impossible to accept the liberal population's rhetoric that they share our love for the USA when their words and actions don't support them.

There may be those who'll attempt to disavow what I have to say here about love and try to pass it off lightly. It'll be a wasted effort because the experience of love is not an uncertain proposition. It was either experienced or it wasn't, and every individual knows deep down inside of him or herself whether or not deep affection and discipline was experienced. Love is a sharing commodity; it must be given as well as received.

EMPTY LOVE

As an unmarried marine in the salacious environment of Shanghai for a year and a half before World War II, I found that there were ample opportunities to engage in worldly pleasures. However, when I joined up, I was going with a girl back home whom I had known for several years and whom I grew to love. Though she was disappointed at my joining the marines (I was out of work and needed a job), she tempered her feelings, and as we parted for the last time, it was with the tacit understanding that I would be striving to get an education by way of the Marine Corps, saving my money, and upon returning home, we would very likely marry, though not in as many words.

At any rate, I intended to conduct myself honorably (as a principled conservative), and all through the early months of my liberty periods in the States, I did so and was able to enjoy myself. I was suffering no hardship by not mingling with the opposite sex, just writing back home a lot. Once I was in China, I began the tour by continuing to stay true to the girlfriend back home. It did grow somewhat awkward, though, continually turning down invitations by marine friends in my billet to double date or share parties with them and their girlfriends, but I continued to enjoy myself on my own and stayed chaste.

There did come an occasion when I was on liberty with a pal and allowed myself to become intoxicated and ended up being seduced by a blowsy prostitute. My feeling afterward was anger, not so much at my buddy who instigated it, as at myself. I felt dirty and ashamed and experienced no pleasure. Later I was advised by a regimental physician that perhaps I shouldn't be such a homebody; being so many thousands of miles away from home-and-family for the first time, perhaps I ought to be out in society more, mixing with my cohorts.

I admit that after that bit of medical advice, there were intimate encounters with girls of my own volition, but each time afterward I had an uncomfortable, dirty feeling, with no sense of deep emotion. Nothing enjoyable or good came of any of the unions, and my conscience really troubled me when I wrote to my sweetheart back home. A hard pill to swallow for this more-or-less sheltered, naïve young man (*to start with*) was the fact that of the six basic needs of human beings, civilization had debased the *basic drive to reproduce* to a level of evil, to carnal pleasure, the pursuit of which ruins lives right and left.

The interval in Shanghai was a rich learning experience about human morality because the International Settlement was populated by millions of Chinese, a mix of refugees of all nationalities (mostly Russians who escaped the revolution) and was a terribly libidinous environment. Girls coached by ambitious mothers would literally throw themselves at young marines in the hope of a marriage and in that way get into America.

Old-timers arriving for a tour of duty in Shanghai were advised to shack up with a female at the start of their tour, if they were of a mind to, so as to have a safe, steady sex partner for the next two years (unless she stepped out on you and incurred a disease). Those sex partners were generally passed on from a marine returning stateside to a newly arrived marine, much as an object of value. The marine was advised to have his partner come to the naval hospital for verification of good sexual health and to have checkups at regular intervals. All were told to avoid having children, and that marriage was out of the question at all times—period.

I think that mixing with my thousand or so cohorts and observing their behavior, as well as that of other people, broadened my youthful knowledge significantly during the time I was in Shanghai. All in all, the societal mix was a seemingly good cross section of liberal *and* conservative types. I learned one basic fact, for sure: *young men tend to want to have brief interludes with girls, whereas girls want to have deep, meaningful relationships with boys of their liking.*

I decided that the inclinations of liberal's tended to lie below the navel, figuratively speaking, while those of the conservatives were largely above the navel, more cerebral as it were, though my subjects were not monk-like individuals or abstainers from sex. It never ceases to amaze me, however, the power of the sex urge.

In another book (unpublished as yet) telling of my service during World War II, I relate how my true love Ruth and I did finally get together in our senior years. After my being reported missing and presumed dead during the war, she married another guy and had a couple of children. Her husband died in 1990 and later in 1995 she made a trip back to Iowa (where I lived) on business and learned that I had made it back home safely from the war. She thought to look me up by way of several phone directories and succeeded. She was widowed, and I was divorced, so we got together, made a pact, and together we're still catching up.

She and I live in our own little world, so to speak, and are happy in it. Being a conservative, however, I deplore the disgusting life Americans are reduced to living because of where liberalism has taken us. American leisure life has lost touch with so much that's good—good music (popular and listening music with melody *and* lyrics), thoughtful television programs, worthwhile movies, good newspapers, good magazines, even good manners and good behavior.

LOVE HER OR HATE HER

Sarah Palin's persona is so interesting that practically everyone wants to express some views about her. From the night of her nomination for vice president when I first saw her come onto the stage with Senator John McCain and her family and then knock the crowd dead with her spirit and her rhetoric, I saw and felt something in her that I hungered to see again. I'm not talking about something physical, though one has to admit she is attractive.

The most outstanding quality that I took away from her debut that night was her wholesomeness, like a breath of fresh air. Here is a young woman that one can tell comes from a loving family. She's a jewel of principled conservatism. Though a mother of five children, she has an almost virginal quality about her with that uncomplicated straightforwardness. She generates in me a feeling that I could kill anyone who would harm a hair of her head. Yet there are many liberals who do not share my opinion, and I worry that there are some who are not above doing her harm. Perhaps that's what sparks this passion in me.

It's curious that the very things so many conservative people like about Palin are precisely what so many liberals do not like, and their negative feelings are about as intense as the conservative's positive feelings. She infuriates huge numbers of liberals, women and men alike, and doubtless it's because of her personal qualities.

She's adored by a large, loving family, as well as by most of the people of Alaska. One cannot escape the fact that she's held significant posts, the governorship of Alaska certainly. That position alone was a far more significant skilled position than any that Barack Obama ever held. She's so level-headed, possessing the kind of qualities that liberal women can't begin to measure up to, and that riles huge numbers. Conservative men and women, in turn, love her for all of the very same reasons.

I feel that she occupies more conservative hearts and souls than any woman in ages. Like me, they're excited by the aura of a young woman who's so capable—a mother, one of her children being handicapped, a woman who's done so many things, been so successful, and an indoor-outdoor woman to boot. Not only does she have a husband and family who truly love her, but she's a lady who wears her charm with a gentle grace and is a Christian.

With the passing of time, the frivolous lawsuits to which she and her husband had been required to respond became so excessively expensive that she had no choice but to resign her governor post to end the suits so as to have something left for grocery money, as it were. It was Alaska's loss.

For what it's worth, it seems that her platform voice and her conversational voice are somewhat different; on the platform, projecting to an audience, she tends to sound a tiny bit shrill, "Fargo-ish…yaaah shure" (Norwegian-ish, like the dialect of my ancestors). Perhaps that's too earthy for the elite type. I find it refreshing. Her conversational voice is pleasingly normal.

She is currently in limbo, but you can bet that down the road, she will certainly be some sort of a factor in the political arena because of her immense popularity. I'm convinced that she has an analytical overview of American issues that very few in politics can equal.

This might be an ideal point in the premise for the reader to perhaps peek into his or her soul and get an idea of which criteria, as enunciated earlier, best fits his or her nature, i.e., conservative or liberal. Sarah Palin being the lightning rod that she is in our society, I ask the reader to consider whether he or she likes or dislikes her. If one can honestly say that he or she likes her, then I would conclude that that person was loved and disciplined during the first five years of his or her life, thus a conservative.

Should one *not* like Sarah Palin, then I'd conclude that that person did not receive the love and discipline that he or she needed during the first five years of life, so that person is of a liberal bent. To that I say, "So what?" Whatever has been done is done; life will go on as usual, and that person will have lots of company. If that person should ever want to convert to conservatism, he or she certainly can do so by giving one's life to Christ.

DAUGHTER, DAUGHTER, QUITE CONTRARY

"Daughter, daughter, quite contrary, how does the
search for a husband go?"
"Mother, dear mother, I'm sleeping around, so how
am I to know?"

All across the fruited plain, there is much gnashing of
teeth on the part of liberal parents who have been overly
permissive and now have reason to be concerned about
the moral character of their daughters, particularly
those parents who scrimped and sacrificed and put all
their assets into a college education for a daughter, only
to realize that they didn't do the child any favor.

Not only did the daughters not get educated necessarily, but they got indoctrinated with off-the-wall ideologies by leftist intellectuals passing themselves off as
professors and they may also have fallen into the prac-

tice of sleeping around because "it's the thing to do" on campus. They could have become part of the morally bankrupt "hookup" culture, wherein a boy and a girl, possibly even strangers, go hand-in-hand to someplace with a bed, and even if there should happen to be others in another bed in the same room, just ignore them and proceed to indulge their sexual appetites, fornicating.

The liberal American girl who sleeps around is, doubtless, vacuous enough to think she's a liberated female, but I sure can't see a young man worth his salt marrying such a girl. What kind of young man would want to father a baby issuing from a pigsty.

It's in the nature of the lovelorn, female liberal who has never known genuine love to chase her own tail in a futile search for it. Anyway, who's responsible? In the first place, it was the parents who were incapable of practicing love and discipline with the child as it grew. The final product: an immature, aimless, adult liberal. This is a classic example of the subject matter in an early chapter of the premise, about television destroying the parent role. In many homes across America, the parents were, and still are, being reduced to being just somebody in the house with the kids. The kids, of course, fashion their behavior from the degenerative examples they see on the tube.

It's doubtless the primary reason why so many female leftists of all ages are slatternly. With liberal influence being in the ascendancy, morals don't seem to matter. Many liberal mothers have plainly abdicated their responsibilities as human beings. They are permissive with their children, get lazy, dissatisfied, grow obese, are uncaring, and, as a consequence, lead empty existences.

It's no wonder that societies around the earth who see nothing but trashy pictures of American girls and hear nothing but bad reports jump to conclusions and have nothing but contempt for our society. Too much of this kind of behavior is glorified in books, movies, soap operas, and on the stage. Fighting off liberal media publicity certainly makes for an uphill battle for young women who want to go straight.

Most married women today almost certainly don't have it as good as the married couples in my day for a lot of different reasons. Because of the country's far larger population, the majority are liberals who understandably have more bad marriages. The majority of the liberal young women will be divorced, estranged, or just flat-out abandoned and spend the bulk of their time working, perhaps at more than one job (should they be fortunate to even be employed) or looking for work. Those who have children are probably able to leave them with a parent or relative if they're lucky, but most probably have to use some sort of babysitting service. In any case, bad things come of that because the child, especially during the first two years of life, needs to be with a parent. At that time the child needs its mother desperately to give it love and discipline and to be its role model.

I hope that young mothers, the ones who have at least a small amount of time on their hands, will not shirk their responsibility. If they should happen to be guilty, they should decide to stop being *nice*; *be a parent, not a friend* to their daughters and make them know that life is a serious matter, that there are things to do and things not to do. Most importantly, it would be in the conservative way to talk to their girls about the fact that life is a serious matter, that they're the mothers of tomorrow and ought to strive to form a plan for their lives, something their mother may not have done well.

When I first entered the music industry after college, women were still held in high esteem. In fact, one of the primary concerns of young women at the time was that of being put on a pedestal by adoring young men. In scanning through some of the treasured song titles of that not so long ago time, it was extremely common to see the use of the girl-directed personal pronoun *you* in song titles, as in "Embraceable You," "The Very Thought of You," "I Love You Truly," "Only You," "I'll Be Seeing You," "You Go to My Head," etc. Just to think, marriages then were founded on *real* love, a romantic kind of love, and they were generally good marriages—*and* between men and women. The divorce rate: extremely low.

I was proud of the fact then that my wife didn't have to leave home to help put bread on the table. She was able to spend her time caring for the children, training them, and keeping up a nice home for the kids and us to share, and we were all happy with the arrangement, as were homemakers in general.

I blame liberalism and deplore those liberal elements that first cast aspersions upon the term *homemakers*, demeaning the family status, thereby initiating the moral slide toward today's ultimate idiocy: I have in mind a slimy television series called *Desperate Housewives*. Did it make money for its producers? Hopefully it didn't. It's a sad, sad commentary on our culture if such perverted material can be made to be profitable.

Anyway, sluttish behavior is not in the nature of today's principled conservative female. With our culture being divided between unprincipled-liberals and principled-conservatives, it's a given that the conservative females are going to have an uphill battle combating an entrenched liberal media, but it's my sense that they're doing a marvelous job of it and, at the same time, keeping the institution of marriage alive. It just isn't in the nature of principled conservative young women to conduct themselves like trollops. Their moral character will not permit it.

America's conservative young women as well as mature women are the most lovely, enchanting, beautiful females in the world, bar none. It should be noteworthy that I used the term *conservative* in identifying the ladies, and that's because *being beautiful outside comes from being beautiful inside,* and conservative women certainly are that. How satisfying to realize that beauty can be an inward thing. This applies to conservative women of all ages, whom by their peaceful, composed inner-nature, radiate an inner beauty. What an inducement that should be to a liberal female to convert to Christi-anity; it's a cosmetic that comes with the change.

I've learned that all of that beauty and quality is not easy to bear. Disturbed, liberal young white *and* men of color stalk lovely young ladies to satisfy their perverted sex drives. The nation is blessed that its young ladies are courageous enough to persevere with their daily lives.

I am particularly impressed with the concept pur-sued by the Clare Booth Luce Policy Institute of Hern-don, Virginia, whose goal is to work closely with large numbers of conservative young women to help them fight back against liberal bias on the nation's college campuses. The nation owes the institute a vote of thanks. Its commitment will significantly assist a body of young women who espouse the conservative way and strive to maintain a pride in America and its young women, despite all the trashy publicity the lovelorn female liber-als generate.

What's more, it's reassuring to us older adults. If the conservative Luce ladies have their way, there will always be a sizeable pool of decent, marriageable girls in society for our sons, grandsons, and great-grandsons to choose from. It goes without saying that parents of today's young men would be well advised to consult with them about the bad and the good of the sex drive so that high-quality young women of tomorrow will have a high-quality pool of young men to choose from for their mates.

We must give a lot of credit to the many young women in the military services. Truth be known, most of the female recruits come from warm, loving homes with conservative parents who got them off on the right foot in life. Most of them will be able to hold their own with vulgar male counterparts and be proud, upstanding feminine soldiers, sailors, marines, and air personnel, plus making good wives.

Doubtless, they enter the service with their eyes wide open and willing to accept whatever it takes to see them through graduation and into the ranks of the regulars. After serving their tour of duty they are likely to be even better, more principled females than when they went in. My hat's off to them, as everyone's should be.

THE RED-BLOODED AMERICAN MALE

"John Wayne, where are you when we need you?"

Besides sports, what do today's young men and boys engage in? Hunting? Maybe a little bit. It's not as easy to get onto property as it used to be. Fishing? Maybe, at least fishermen can get to good fishing spots easier than hunters can get onto good hunting land. The good old days of tinkering with cars has pretty much gone down the tube, unless one has an older car. Most boys used to get dirty and sweaty, messing around with their cars and motorcycles after school, but now it seems that the majority of those I see are wearing tees and looking clean. That's probably because they're messing around with their Lamborghini or their I-Pad or what have you.

Surely young women who have spirit would like their male counterparts to have spirit also, to be red-blooded guys, wouldn't they? After all, who likes a namby-pamby? Being red-blooded doesn't mean a guy is a rapist or some overpowering individual, as some would have that to mean. I know conservative young men who I would call red blooded who are perfect gentlemen where females are concerned. I would think that any girl worth her salt should be able to cope with today's young men anyway.

I worry that because of parents being overly cautious, too protective, and spending too much time together (this is possible and becomes a real problem if siblings are still living at home at age twenty-one), there seems to be a reticence at raising virile, spirited young men. Regrettably, we seem to be raising a generation of mild-mannered young men (mostly liberals) who lack the traditional male characteristics—leadership, having a spirit of derring-do, courageous, husky, willing to stand up to bullies, able to make decisions, able to withstand criticism, being protective of the weak, etc.

It concerns me that the military is having trouble meeting their quotas of the kinds of recruits that they'd like. They're finding much of the field of prospects too fat, poorly motivated, and not well educated. This spells big trouble down the road unless the trend is reversed soon. The fact that there are so many liberal educational institutions that won't allow military recruiters on their grounds is a serious handicap and of grave concern. I think that some form of brief military draft for the able-bodied would be good for the country and its young men.

Mothers surely mean well, but in recent years, they have been profoundly influenced by liberal women's groups who tend to want everybody to be alike, straying from individualism in the process. They advocate that young men should conform, to not make waves; apparently that way they make more docile, manageable husbands. As a consequence, many men have had their masculinity and individuality taken from them, for which the country is paying a high price. Witness the inability of men in high places to make hard decisions today.

Mothers and fathers (even if liberals) would do well to butt-in and try to spruce up their student sons. There's too much dark, baggy clothing, poor posturing, and a lack of personal pride that is established by peer-pressure and celebrity-influence. How about the bill cap worn sideways or backward—and wearing it inside of the building. (Whatever happened to that male practice of removing the headgear?)

I suggest that a real, honest-to-goodness virtual reality program is needed; that members of society, particularly women, should make it a point to observe the nature of birds and water fowl. They are monogamous, and humans can learn one heck of a lot about reality and nature from them. Viewing at the zoo is not the kind of venue I had in mind. I suggest going to a *big* city park or better still, to a state park.

There are a lot of consequences of widespread *liberal motherhood failure* showing up in society. Many among the recent generations of young male left-ists are showing disappointing masculine behavior. It's manifesting itself in effeminacy, stalking behavior, child predatory behavior, homosexuality, unassertiveness, self-consciousness, timidity, incompetence, hesitancy, impotency, thin voice, weak-countenance, tattooing, body piercing, scruffy beard (far too widespread), long hair, braided hair, bandana about the head, no tie/open-collared shirts (the unprofessional look), etc. It's all indicative of insecurity, fear, a lack of self-worth, self-confidence, and self-respect. The majority of embellishments amount to an attempt to appear macho and virile, a psychologist would recognize it as stemming from a basic lack of inner strength.

The copious measure of filthy blogging one finds on the Internet is directly due to scads of irresponsible, faceless male liberals and radicals. They have a typical emptiness that causes them to also be drawn to violence and morbidity. Crimes of late suggest that the dysfunctional mind in both men and women is extremely dangerous, making them capable of hatching the most heinous of crimes.

It's my opinion that young conservative men and women of the future ought to make good choices and genuinely fall in love, marry early, and plan on having large families so that once more America can build up the virility of its Yankee stock, as it were.

Dare I say it, "We need some balls around here."

SICKNESS IN
THE CITY

Wow! Those bright lights at night sure are attractive and inviting from an aircraft...or from space. Then comes daylight; one sees the landscape for what it is—a seething mass of civilization: cars, trucks, motorcycles, bicycles, emergency vehicles, and, oh, that mass of people, and receptacles of trash. Everything and everybody moving, going somewhere, until traffic gets jammed; then one must live with horns and whistles and shouts until the traffic gets to moving and settles into a steady roar again.

The people in sight: ordinary laborers, executives, office workers, truck drivers, policemen, tourists, firemen, delivery men, etc. Then there are people not working: panhandlers, pensioners, welfare recipients, the aimless, and the homeless. We're talking about downtown, of course. At the end of the day, most all of those people, but the homeless, are going to residences close by or out to the suburbs in cars and city transit for the night, losing hours of living in the process of getting there. Then the coming-and-going process will be repeated the next working day, and more hours of living are lost. And so it is with the rat race in the big city.

Life in the city gets even more disquieting at the city-on-the-bay, the northern leg of California's "Sodom and Gomorrah," Hollywood being the southern leg. There are decent working people in San Francisco just as in other cities but not only do they have to put up with toll bridges   and hills, but with a radical, liberal attitude among the city administration that hates any kind of *morality or goodness*. It even defies America's armed forces, whom they might have to call on to save their rear someday. It's an evil, immoral, indecent city. It defies the imagination to think that any patriotic conservative citizen could live there.

Hollywood may not have to put up with toll bridges, but its decent residents have to put up with the same kind of blight: a cynical attitude toward evil and immorality among its population of entertainers. The overwhelmingly liberal entertainment industry displays not even a little bit of outward decency in the community as it dispenses violence and indecent filth to a literally brain-dead market.

I see the ugliness of evil so much now, it's almost becoming commonplace. Because I am conservative by nature, thus motivated by beauty and achievement, I am overjoyed when I can witness ecstatic pleasure showing on an individual's face that comes with something being achieved. If liberals could just realize the powerful sense of satisfaction and pleasure that comes with being part of things positive. Alas, from what one is learning about the daisy-dandelion concept, one knows that enjoying something positive is next to impossible for a liberal.

I wonder why anyone would want to live in a metropolis if one could help it. The noise is bad; the air is bad; the traffic is bad; and space is limited. And besides that, people just don't seem to have the time to be decent to each other. One supposes that in the city it's only during the workday in shops, offices, warehouses, cubicles, Starbucks, and the like that those humans get to behave sort of normally for any length of time. I swear, God just didn't ordain life to be as complex as it is in a major city.

Considering elements of the daisy-dandelion concept, the fact that liberals and conservatives *do* coexist alongside each other at work in close quarters in a city is a blessing, and something for conservatives and liberals alike to digest. That kind of working relationship bodes well for America's future.

Another unique thing about liberalism is the high number of black mayors, chiefs of police, and council members in large cities where blacks are not in the majority. It has the look and sound of lazy white people saying, "Let somebody else do it." That kind of racial imbalance in a city's top echelons, probably inspired by a combination of indifference, the Democratic Party, and affirmative action, makes for one heck of a lot of problems, not the least of which is an unjustified lordly mien adopted by some liberal blacks in positions of authority.

It's the major cities that have the most serious financial problems and where, by the way, are some of the deepest cost-cuts in the cities made? Why, in police departments and libraries, of course. May we hope and pray that the Electoral College, which takes into consideration regional characteristics across the nation as opposed to huge concentrations of people in a few enormous cities in presidential elections, is never changed.

There is a huge disconnect when 40 percent or more of the population pays no taxes and then lives on another wage earner's money paid in taxes. It's not logical for governmental agencies to be overly concerned about physically able people who make no contribution to society, not even performing community service in many cases.

Taxpayer money is properly spent on a community's infrastructure, not charity. The private sector is always generous with its support of the needy, so nobody is going to suffer as a consequence of not being paid with taxpayer dollars. If not employed, the able-bodied should, at all times, be involved in some sort of community service effort to the community he or she lives in. For a society not to do this is not only a disservice to the individual, demeaning him or her to the level of a deadbeat, but it's insulting to regular wage earners who drive the engine of prosperity.

SOPHISTRY FROM THE BULLY PULPIT

Sophistry: subtly deceptive reasoning or argumentation.
A sophist is known for adroit, subtle and spacious
reasoning; a captious or fallacious reasoning.

Webster's Dictionary

It'll be to the everlasting shame of the mindless Democrat electorate of 2008 who went to the polls in lockstep, like lemmings plunging over a cliff, that managed (but not by much) to elect an unvetted man to the nation's highest office, most of whom will never, ever have the courage to admit to their bungle. It will go down in history as an electorate of uninformed leftist fools who thought perhaps that in Obama they had a nemesis, a power who might suppress all of the goodness in America that so infuriates them. He would be their protective shield, able to destroy or halt the threat to them of all the conservative-aggravations from across the land:

the do-gooders, the older generation, the tea baggers, morality, the discomforting voices coming across the air waves from radio and cable television, etc.

Those electors foolishly attached a messianic mien to Barack Obama as they chorused for change. If they harbored thoughts of something noble coming of their gullibility, like presuming the first black president would be a giant of character, capable of making America the most radical nation in the world and its leader, they were in for a rude awakening.

Actions have consequences, and this one was asked for as the blind led the blind to the polls. The consequence was a new president who is dangerous to the nation's health, being of a radical Progressive bent. Notice those with whom he surrounds himself. Besides, he seems to be shallow, lacking in depth of character. Limitedly experienced in the political or business arena, he is a victim of a broken home, enormously immature at forty-seven, with credentials woefully unbefitting the highest office in the land.

A long, hard look at the election scenario smacks of long-range planning from the far left, the strings undoubtedly pulled by way of the wealth of George Soros. The timing was excellent for the new administration, as the lame duck presidency of George W. Bush had its hands more than full in the war with the terrorists, the Democrat's *control of both houses of congress* "ham stringing" him and the Fannie Mae housing debacle getting way out of hand.

President Obama also brought into office with him an underhanded administration that once safely ensconced in office put what appeared to be a plan into place to rape the national treasury and to thumb its nose at the Constitution in an effort to provide some redress to minority Americans for alleged long suffering at the expense of capitalism. The administration seems to feel comfortably safe from penalty, presuming that white Americans don't like to be called racists.

After experiencing a couple years of the president's behavior, the collective actions of his associates Eric Holder (who reminds one of Janet Reno) and Valerie Jarrett from whom Obama may get his daily "marching orders", suggest a malevolence not unlike that of Satan and his apostate angels. Among their leftist's creed(s) which have been passed down through the years from communists, fascists, progressives, socialists, etc. are "whatever it takes the end will justify the means" and "never fail to take advantage of a good crisis."

Collectively, the new administration has made it very plain that it will say what's expedient, even if it's a lie; it will not bow to public opinion or parliamentary procedure, and apologies are not in the administration's lexicon. At heart it is composed of several distressed, angry liberal progressives who get perverse pleasure at sticking their collective fingers into the eyes of the public. All must have had troubled, uncaring parents and miserable childhoods. *They're dandelions for sure.*

It appears that the White House has the look, the smell, of an oligarchy. By definition, an oligarchy is a small segment of society, very powerful, whether by wealth, military strength, ruthlessness, or political influence. Instead of the president being surrounded by an armed military, as would usually be the case, there are czars already in place. They are there unconstitutionally, of course.

For openers, there was a sortie flaunting the Constitution, a many-paged stimulus bill tying up 780 billion dollars of the nation's wealth allowed to be hustled through two supposedly responsible but liberally controlled bodies of Congress under the guise of "an emergency facing the American economy so desperate that there'd be no time to read it in either house."

The tomfoolery came about even though the new president had, as a candidate, promised at least five days of transparency on all bills once he was elected, one of the first of many, many, *many* sophist-type deceptions to follow. The monstrosity was powered through the democratically controlled Congress in seventy-two hours, and not a single Congressman got a look at the contents, the image of the President of the United States emerging as a real-life despot. It left one aghast and feeling dirty, not unlike what a woman must feel after being raped.

Considering the enormity of the action that actually succeeded, the American public should never forget how gullible and gutless the Democratic majority, in fact, the *whole five hundred and forty members of the 111th Congress* behaved. It's rather obvious that Obama and his administration have nothing but contempt for the IQ of Congress *and* the American people, and considering the judgment of the liberals who put the administration into office, I can see why.

President Obama is never at a loss for words or perplexed by a "gotcha" question but that he can fend it away and turn it on the questioner, suggesting that he'd already done something about whatever it was or able to blame it on the George W. Bush presidency. Apparently he doesn't have it in him to be able to accept a dissenting view.

The president is not only a smooth talker, but he has evidently mastered the art of sophistry, an ancient art, the thrust of which is to deceive an adversary with twisted logic. *He is certainly succeeding at perplexing the nation with it. (Obama once took seventeen minutes to answer a question he was hard-pressed to answer.)*

Apparently President Obama is also employing sophistry to make economic statistics that are deplorable *look good. Anymore, at our house, when we see Obama appearing on television, we depress the mute switch.*

Since leopards don't change their spots, it isn't likely that the president and his people will stop lying or end deceptive practices or quit skirting the Constitution.

There are so many irregularities being recklessly breezed past the American people right now that one can't help but get a nauseous feeling in the pit of one's stomach.

There's not much the conservative public can do about the situation, though, but bide one's time until victory comes about in the ballot box and the administration surely knows it. One can bet that the Democrat clique there in Camelot gets a large-charge out of watching frustrated conservatives publicly fret and fume.

I take comfort in knowing that *for each of them, there will come a time* when he or she will have to account to his or her Maker. Perhaps each will be judged on whether or not the part each played in the governance of America was unselfish and for the good of the nation.

Once the liberal Obama administration's seeming racially motivated conduct is seen for what it is, it could have the potential of setting back racial gains made in America for years, and it may already be starting. I would think conservative African Americans wouldn't want that to happen.

For much of my life, the impressions I had gotten of African Americans from what I saw in the news were aggravating, in fact, maddening. I didn't want to admit to it, but I actually thought myself to be racist. Then I discovered that there were *principled* conservative African Americans who had had good parenting and shared the same kind of mindsets as I, used logic like me, etc. *Those other African Americans making the bad impressions were hateful liberals* who'd had bad parenting and had grown up with chips on their collective shoulders.

I was pleased to learn that there is a large segment of the African-*American* population that is well educated, conservative and happy to be called good Americans, "daisies," just like me and other principled conservatives. There is another large segment of African American society though that is composed of hateful liberals, just as there is a huge, radical, hateful segment of white liberals with chips on their shoulders..

A tragic misreading of history could be in the works because during the Civil War the northern states were anti-slavery, sympathetic to the slave's cause, providing underground railroads and other assistance to help free them. It was the plantation owners in the relatively few Southern states who actually bartered and traded slaves that couldn't accept the fact that the war was over and that the Confederacy had lost, thereby causing them to take out their hate on the ex-slaves who chose to stay in the South.

That hateful attitude manifest by the segregation of blacks existed in those Southern states all through the years to the time of Rosa Parks and the sit-ins. It concerns me that the sympathy for the slave's cause in the many friendly northern states during the Civil War appears to have been largely forgotten by those African Americans who are hate-consumed. *People of the northern states shouldn't be tarred by the same brush that tars the shameful South, which President Lincoln and the north engaged in a civil war over for, of all things, the abolition of slavery.*

Worrisome is the haste with which the treasury is being drained, the consequence being valueless currency. When that happens, it's likely that the conservative middle class, which has always been the backbone of America, will be a thing of the past. Unless spending is arrested soon, that tragedy could be near.

Further clouding the sordid picture is the fact that the president has made no secret of his leanings toward a global society. His journeys about the globe have demonstrated that he has no particular loyalty to America or love for it, although his Harvard law connection and writings have made him some capitalist money. His lackluster résumé shows him as having been a neighborhood organizer in Chicago and having had a partial term as a U.S. senator from Illinois.

He has traveled about the world, apologizing for what he openly refers to as past American aggression and vindictiveness, boasting of his Muslim connections (I possess a televised tape of ten minutes or so in length on which he goes to great length to glorify his Muslim credentials), though he claims to be Christian, and is anxious to earn friends and relationships for the administration. So far, the fruits of apologizing for America's glory days seem not to have done him a lot of good, witness Copenhagen.

He doesn't hide his disdain for America's past exceptionalism, nor does he hide his pleasure at the prospect of the USA becoming a welfare state. His tribal ancestry, with its inherent resentment toward the white man, shows through on occasion; it's obvious that he would be pleased to have America transformed into a socialist state. Obama, like Al Sharpton, Jesse Jackson, Rev. Wright and Louis Farrakhan, appears to have no desire to better the status of impoverished blacks, rather keeping them subservient to their black masters. Obama's tacit indulgence in this farce speaks volumes.

The president has an ingratiating manner that he habitually uses with individuals from whom he would curry favor, manifesting itself with an arm being draped about the accompanying person's shoulder or by contact through a touch or grasp of the other party's back or arm. Perhaps the president doesn't realize that it's an offensive gesture; it's a violation of one's personal space, overly familiar, unless one invites the gesture. He seems to have no knowledge of protocol—or he just doesn't give a darn.

The president's daily appearances on television suggest that he might have a streak of vanity about him, or perhaps it is part of a master plan designed to keep his person before certain segments of his electorate. One often gets the feeling that he'd rather be out shooting baskets than fulfilling the office of the presidency. It's hard to shake the feeling that he's naught but a figurehead president.

The directions the Democrats and the president are taking constitute a real and present danger to the future of America. There is no illegality involved, but there'd just as well be, considering how the constitution is being pummeled in Washington.

One can put absolutely no stock in the president's deceitful sophist-speak, and way too many conservatives are still giving Obama the benefit of the doubt. They just shake their heads, trying to make sense of what he is doing and saying. They shouldn't hold their breath, for *it's not in the nature of a sophist* to be honest and straightforward. He is deceptive — period. People might want to do as we do at home when he appears on television, i.e., click the mute button. One of these days, the man may be charged with malfeasance in office and impeached.

CRY ME A RIVER

Conditions in the country, to me, are bad enough to paraphrase the old Julie London record hit "Cry Me a River" and may, in fact, justify "Cry Me a Whole Darned Ocean." Explaining why society is in the mess it's in, lies within the scope of the daisy-dandelion theorem.

If the administration in power is the nation's most serious current lament, there are at least five other matters close behind that will require crying towels when discussing them. Number one among them is education.

For a major change to happen with education, it will be essential for a new administration coming into power to agree that it warrants extraordinary action. Ideally, a new cabinet post would be created, *taking precedence over all others*, simply because America's youth and how it grows-up should be made a matter of top-drawer importance on the agenda of every future administration taking office.

Parenting is so serious an issue that a course in it should be made part of every state's educational curriculum. An in-depth textbook should be compiled—one that's free of ideology and another *like* book made available for putting in the hands of all newly married couples. Further, legislation should be adopted making parents responsible for the care and behavior of their children. That clause should be made inescapable. After all, it's because of a parent's actions whenever there is a new face in society.

This will be a subject of intense differences of opinion. Tempers will flare, and cool heads will be needed to prevail and to control debate. Intrusion upon privacy will be the biggest issue, but the seriousness of the subject matter must not be allowed to be sidetracked or diminished by emotional argumentation. A major obstacle to change will be the teacher's union, which must not be allowed to exist. Staff and teachers should be compensated on the basis of merit. There should be ongoing reviews between parents and teachers requiring attendance by at least one of the parents.

An equally major lament that defies resolve is the widespread use of mood-altering substances—everything from alcohol to methamphetamines, to marijuana, to heroin, etc. The super huge cost in dollars and "sense" due to drug, alcohol, and marijuana use never shows up in statistics like other costs do. Why is that? Were those costs to be made public as often as those of the *military* wouldn't Congress and the people then be more anxious to end *their* use?

To me, correction of the problem is sort of a chicken-or-the-egg proposition. Where does one start? Does one address the beginning of the problem with the individual or the problem at the end where a huge portion of society is hooked (user Americans numbering in the millions) and the nation that has all the users is in collision at the border with the country where the "candy" comes from? The answer, of course, is that the problem must be simultaneously addressed at both ends. This will be a *supremely challenging issue* for a new administration, considering the large numbers in society that are users.

From my position, championing the daisy-dandelion theorem, I fully understand why a young person introduces him or herself, or accepts introduction from someone else, to usage of any kind of mood altering substance(s). *It stems from faulty parenting.* I am confident that initial experimentation is *brought on by inner emptiness,* fostered by a host of negative personal issues that collectively balloon to a point beyond which an individual sees no alternatives. He or she finally sees no incentive to discourage experimenting with a substance that might make one feel good, and so he or she becomes a ready prospect for the drug pusher.

All young children are in a hurry to grow up, and they enjoy mimicking their parents and relatives. If individuals in the family smoke, imitation will not be far behind, likewise with liquor. If beer or other alcoholic beverages are being consumed, the minor is going to feel comfortable with using them when he or she is of age (or maybe sooner). Later on, the flushed sense that comes with intoxication will cause one to drop his or her barriers of resistance to sex, narcotics, etc., so one might easily embark on a lifetime of immorality and all the negative consequences that follow.

Of singular concern in California is the pressure on the general public and legislators to eliminate all resistance to the unrestricted use of marijuana. It's been one of those things for a long time, where on the one hand there are licensed pot shops that operate under the aegis of medicinal benefit only, but anyone shopping for it will have no trouble procuring it.

I am convinced that it is a substance which, over time, will cook the brain, good ol' boy arguments to the contrary. Consequently, it leaves the non-user uncomfortable and concerned when individuals in prestigious positions snicker or joke about "a little weed, cannabis, hemp, or whatever." They seem to derive larcenous pleasure at being comedic about a subject that aggravates *California's public, which seems to be largely straight.*

At the other end of the issue lies another huge problem. It manifests itself in a most distressing way, at the United States border with Mexico. There, desperate people with no regard for human life kill each other daily, in some cases by beheadings, to either acquire drugs or for control of marketing the substance(s) so desperately needed by the hooked American users.

Another terribly serious issue for the nation to face is that of unions. There is need for immediacy in addressing the seriousness of their influence on the nation's well being.

I need not go into detail to remind a reader how powerful the union entities are all across the country in manufacturing, transportation, correctional institutions, education, services, entertainment, municipalities, etc., etc. When the individual is taken out of the employer-employee equation, the employer is put at a distinct advantage and so is the employee. The organization or parent whose capital it is that keeps the engine running, is forced to contend with a well-financed entity that has no further agenda than to extort money and concessions from *it*, under the pretense of providing harmony with its employees. To me, it's a socially sanctioned form of blackmail that should be outlawed at the earliest possible opportunity. There have to be more acceptable means available for negotiating differences between an employer and its employees than the monstrously expensive and gangster-like methods currently in vogue.

✻

A constant source of wonderment is whatever happened to the media? A person hears that question constantly. I long for newspapers and the reporting of yesteryear plus the integrity that was part of the genre. The reporters one sees in the pressroom at the White House now tend to give the Democratic administration the benefit of any doubts, so I see their publications as being the propaganda arm of the government.

Obvious is the intimidated behavior of the press corps as they face the more ill-humored responses of Obama and his people, as opposed to that of the better-mannered President Bush and his people. The fawning atmosphere in the press-room, during interviews and Q&A sessions with President Obama and his Press Secretary is offensive to watch. One finds it hard to dismiss from the mind how two-faced and insulting they were to George Bush, a president who was a decent man.

In the print media, there are a couple of daily papers and perhaps several more that operate journalistically—one being the conservative *Wall Street Journal*, another *The Investors Business Daily*. What one sees and reads in them is factual—not so with *The New York Times* and other liberal, family-owned chains of papers and periodicals which have ideological agendas and are primarily in the business for the advertising revenues. Fox News, on cable television, does strive to be fair and balanced in its reporting of the news, though some of its male anchors squire a much too self-important demeanor in inserting their vanity into segments outside the scope of their positions.

Private investment in locally owned and operated newspapers, radio, and television stations all across the country should be encouraged and at all costs. An important lesson to be learned from experience is that communities with populations of from several thousand to cities of a million or so, having a local business that is succeeding, must never at any cost allow that business to escape the community.

According to Webster's Dictionary, pornography is material that depicts erotic behavior and is intended to cause sexual excitement.

Porn has become so commonplace and so available in the many adult book stores and the Internet that even some mail-order catalogs do not hesitate to advertise the sale of one or more upscale pornographic CDs and DVDs under the guise of learning, sanctioned by an educational institute. It follows that the porn product is available to anyone who places an order. There is always a disclaimer stating that to buy, one should be an adult, but who's checking?

Statistics on pornography viewing are not readily available, so one is left to speculate as to what percentage of the viewing public are actually frequent viewers, occasional viewers or seldom viewers. When making a judgment from random information, porn's liberal viewing audience is far too big and the public far too ill-informed about how the usage breaks down for age, gender, location, etc. It's hard to know how much of it is falling into the hands of teenagers, which is worrisome. It is without question a debilitating cancer in the body of American society. It's out of the realm of usage by decent principled conservatives, but it's going to be up to them to help put the brakes on this perverse blight if a new and conservative administration comes into office in 2012.

The disgust I feel as I often reflect upon America's descent into mediocrity brings to mind a memory of a news story following the election of 2000 that ended Bill Clinton's tenure and brought George W. Bush into office. It was reported that Bill Clinton's people, upon leaving, had trashed the Oval Office.

What stuck in my craw was the report that a lot of the trash left scattered about were tapes of pornography. At the time, I thought it was not surprising, considering the fact that the ex-president had had his sexual liaison with Monica Lewinsky right there in that office. The historic office had, for a while, been turned into a den of iniquity by a bunch of perverts. I think I'm joined by many who wonder what's going on in that office right *now*.

I'm not proud to admit that I'm no stranger to evil, though I am once again getting right with God, so the memory about the Bill Clinton and his staff has given rise to wonderment and suspicion in me about how extensive the pornography plague in American industry might be today.

I can attest that an interest in pornography is terribly addictive. To me, viewing a porn tape scrambles one's thought-process for awhile, perhaps days. It's not something that one can just simply shut out of one's mind, presto. Should it become necessary to engage in a serious train of thought right away, struggling with lasting, lustful images will make it impossible.

Pornography indulged in solitarily is bad enough, but should one participate in viewing with a group of men, or worse yet, of mixed gender, the spectacle becomes even more depraved and degenerate, and should it occur during working hours, like in an office, then it even becomes a criminal act. Should any of such a depraved group be married, consider the extra baggage that that sick mind has to take home with him or her.

Why can ingenuity and brilliance be easily found in small American businesses that have to innovate to survive, yet at the happening of something like the oil spill in the gulf, for the longest time neither a monstrous corporation like BP, nor the president of the United States could come up with any satisfactory solution to the mess? So, for me, hard-to-understand behavior, unexplainable behavior, or just weird or strange behavior whether in a boardroom, in an office, or even in Washington, leads me to suspect that pornography and drugs are present to some degree every day, both in industry and the government.

Pornography is never going to be a problem in small businesses where livelihoods are at stake, but as for bigger businesses where large numbers of restless young men with troubled minds are in close proximity with each other, I'd be suspicious. I'd like to see 'boardroom warriors' come into being who would prowl the halls of commerce to ferret out the depravity that I believe is present there.

I don't know when illegals started coming over the border from Mexico because it never used to be a problem. It was simple for both Americans and Mexicans to go back and forth at legitimate crossing points in cities and towns on the border. It has apparently been since the destitute of Mexico started coming across the border illegally finding it easy to accomplish, then finding employment in the produce fields of California that migrant ID has become an issue.

Israel has done well with an impenetrable fence around its borders, so I think the United States should make every effort to hurry and finish ours, if for no other reason than to protect our ranchers whose lands border Mexico. Besides their properties being overrun, they are being personally attacked by the illegal Mexican immigrants coming into the USA, trafficking drugs, or looking for work that our own people won't do. The federal government is doing nothing to help the property owners, so the situation has deteriorated to a point of desperation for them *and* the border patrol officers.

The flow of illegal immigrants coming across the United States' extensive border is building to a terribly serious problem because of the lack of money. The state of California is basically bankrupt and still they come, taking advantage of free services at emergency rooms and their babies born here becoming American citizens. (This well-intentioned law must be repealed.)

Once inside the USA, sadly they tend to become "deadbeats", continuing to talk their native language and taking everything we give them, including financial help and service at emergency rooms free of charge. They really are a crop of "dandelions." Reassuring is the attitudes of naturalized Mexican Americans, though, who seem very proud to be American citizens, daisies as it were.

One cannot stress enough how out of balance America is in the grip of a liberal youth culture today. So much of that culture is radical, committing revolting and hideous crime. There's so much crime that some days one feels like being on the *Titanic* in a field of icebergs. Ordinary crime is much more prevalent in the major cities, of course, but incidents of hideous and revolting crime are showing up everywhere across the country, grisly evidence of the fact that the number of dangerously disturbed individuals is increasing at an alarming pace everywhere.

Worrisome is the trend nationwide toward cutting back on police officers and all first responders. Each step taken to reduce our first responders is a step closer to anarchy in the streets. Action should be taken to target prospective troubled youth earlier in their lives as well as closeted-adults. The daisy-dandelion concept could be helpful here. Legislation must finally confront the issue of privacy, the eight-hundred-pound gorilla preventing meaningful crime prevention measures from being taken.

It's gotten to a point where children and young women everywhere are hardly safe to move around out in public. Legislators, for any number of reasons, prison crowding for one, continue to allow sexual offenders to live out their lives in society, to continue committing their heinous crimes. No one is available to watch them constantly so it's my feeling that *chemical castration* is a step which should be on the nation's crime-prevention agenda.

Prisons have serious liberal issues, not the least of which is dealing with the correctional officer's union (union again), whose members are extremely well paid. There are racial conflicts, influences from the outside exercising control inside, and the repair of the "damaged goods" (inmates) is not going well. There seems to be a lot of room for improvement in prisons in general. If I had my way, I'd turn the prison system over to the marines.

Because there is some shame attached to it, obesity is too often falsely characterized as a glandular problem when it's really a matter of self-control and coping with a world of outside influences. The obese condition has become a matter of some significance by way of the airline industry in passenger seating and understandably so. I am averse at seeing excessive fat on any person, and on peace-officers or uniformed-individuals in particular. Since it's so repulsive to see and has become such a common sight, it is an issue that demands immediate national attention. This is a dandelion problem for sure.

AMERICA:
A VICTIM OF
TROUBLED PARENTS

Though I originally intended this premise to be a discourse on people with right-leaning ideologies—conservatives (daisies)—and those with left-leaning ideologies—liberals, radicals, and progressives (dandelions), but it's really come down to being about *good people* and *troubled people*.

I feel the need to remind the reader that this discourse is based on the premise that the first five years of a child's life are critical to its mental and physical development. On the one hand, parents who bring a child into the world and then give it love and discipline will, except for unforeseen circumstances, produce a young adult respectful of authority; one who'll not usually rebel as a teenager and will become a principled conservative, *basically a good person*. On the other hand, parents, or even a single parent, who bring a child into the world and do not provide love and discipline or should *cause it to sense it's not wanted* during the first five years of its life, will produce a young adult whose psyche is scarred and will be, though not necessarily a *bad person*, one who will be, at a minimum, *a troubled one*.

When all is said and done, the positive biblical principles embodied in the conservative's *persona* typifies him or her as an *obvious* good person. For a principled conservative to be something other than a good person, he or she would have to deliberately deviate from the norm.

As for the liberal, the scars left on his or her psyche from parental shortcomings incurred during infancy and early youth cause him or her to be troubled, some to being extremely radical and dangerous, but *all* resentful to some degree toward conservatives. There may possibly be many liberals who have been love-deprived to some degree at infancy yet have principles, who tend to be *good people*, but because they vacillate they just can't quite be labeled principled-conservative. Perhaps they are "conserverals", a blend of conservative/liberal.

Probably the *most* significant entity of troubled minds in the country is the Democrats, and perhaps a few Republicans, in Congress. Ever since they traumatized the Republicans during the Clinton impeachment trial, the Democrats appear to have become deliberately hateful of the right as they willy-nilly spend the common folk's money.

Nowhere is evidence of the troubled mind more obvious than in the House of Representatives among members of the black caucus. Judging from their actions on the Hill, they are seen as high-handed and overbearing. As a clique they must be very hard to get along with. The Charlie Rangel and Maxine Waters matters, not to mention the overbearing behavior of Sheila Jackson Lee are classic examples of crowding the system. Typical of someone with an overblown sense of importance, the black politicians, seemingly, more so than the whites (who are bad enough), tend to let any measure of authority go to their head and get pushy trying to lord it over milder-mannered cohorts.

After the 2010 election when the Republicans took control of the house-of-representatives, Democrat Rep. Hoyer was forced to drop-back a notch. That caused Jim Cleyburn to have to drop-back from that position. It had had some prestige about it and also provided a vehicle for one's personal use, which he now lost. After his loud protests and some concern about Afro-anger, an ill-defined position was especially-created for him by the Democrat leadership whereby he might have some prestige and a provided vehicle. I have yet to see a *modest* Afro-American in Congress.

By-far the *largest group* of troubled minds in the country is the welfare culture. (This collection represents a lot of *bad parenting*.) I don't know how the conglomerate breaks down by race or gender, but long on numbers are *African Americans, illegal immigrants,* and *non-working whites.* The large majority, of course, are going to be liberals. This group, 40 percent-plus of the population could, in time, sink the ship of state because most will turn out to be deadbeats, unproductive individuals who take everything and produce nothing but problems. They resent conservatives, seeing them as their enemy, particularly at election time, who would try to take away all of their goodies.

In an earlier chapter, I made reference to the Amish people, describing them as principled people. Based on what we see and know of them, their conduct is built around *family and love and discipline,* just as the typical principled conservative's family is. The Amish society is composed of peaceful people who mind their own business, are distant to outsiders, and self-sufficient. They are communal by nature. They tend to resent government intrusion, preferring to go it alone, as it were. The Quaker society is somewhat similar in nature to the Amish, and both have earned the label *pacifistic.*

The two societies, both peaceful and self-sufficient, are not pressured in any way for support of the military services. Liberals in society might wonder, since conservatives profess to be principled, hence peaceful, how can they find an accord with violence? A person who studies martial arts doesn't take the art so that he or she can clobber people; it's to learn the art of defending one's self, a purely defensive measure.

So has it always been with America down through the years. The USA has never started a war, but when pushed, it has never flinched, taking the fight to the opponent to win. Despite what the naysayers say about the Iraq War, evidence continues to mount that President Bush did the right thing when responding to the terrorist attack of 9/11 by taking-out Hussein and then laboring to plant a democracy smack dab in the middle of the Middle East. It's a comfort to see democracy taking hold there in the middle-east.

Once the Shiite and the Sunni differences are resolved in the Iraqi parliament, the killings ought to stop. An Iraq democracy is a feather in America's cap, and we citizens have a lot to be proud of, to the chagrin of millions of detractors at home and abroad. I'm not absolutely confident of it, but I have a sense that the American Muslim population, on balance, *is* exerting a positive influence against terrorist sympathetic elements here at home.

A TICKET TO RIDE

Never shall I forget the time I got my social security card and how proud I was of it. It was right after graduating from high school, and I got a job feeding chunks of limestone into a stone crusher, then trucking the particles to farmer's fields to apply, at fifty cents an hour. The next card in my life wasn't really a card—it was printed on a card—but it was a railroad pass. My dad was a railroad section foreman, and a consequence of that was that our entire family had the privilege of riding on any passenger train on the railroad for which he worked free of charge and at any time, except in first-class accommodations. He got personal passes for me and my sisters, so we didn't have to use his and Mom's pass while traveling back and forth on a 'local' to school in the city, ten miles away.

After that came the driver's license, the library card, the savings account card, etc., a wallet full, so to speak. This being a law-and-order society, it was important to carry one's proper identification cards, and that's the way I've always known the United States to be. Today one has to be very careful not to have one's ID stolen.

Some years ago I was fortunate to catch a portion of an interview being conducted on television with the mother of the then rising comic star Chris Rock. I don't recall how they got on the subject, but I recall Chris Rock's mother commenting that there was a lot of black trash in America and a lot of white trash as well. I would like to have been able to compliment her personally on her sagacity as I, for one, certainly agreed with her observation. The more I thought about the "trash" aspect, which can be explained by the daisy-dandelion theorem, the wider the scope became.

Would it not be likely, based on just the law-of-averages, that every ethnic group in every nation on earth would have both good and bad parents. There must be good parents everywhere capable of giving the time it takes during the first five years of their child's lives to raise them-up on a regimen of love and discipline, that they might be better prepared to venture out into the schools of their respective societies, fortified with contentment, inner-strength and self-control? It may be a lot harder to do in the Muslim societies because of unique law, religion, custom, and, of course, the availability of education, but it would be reassuring to the rest of the world's people to know that Muslim parents were also raising-up their children on a regimen of love-and-discipline.

In America, the descendants of the slaves have had two centuries to shake off their tribalism, though it appears from time to time that not all of them have done so. In the course of watching the televised church services of a Baptist church in Atlanta each Sunday, I take great comfort in seeing the large number of African Americans sitting and standing alongside white worshipers in the huge congregation, all harmoniously digesting the Christian message.

It's comforting to see, as it assures one that there are great numbers of blacks in society who are Christian, born and raised by principled parents just like white principled conservatives. I think it's worth mentioning, because it seems that neither television nor the print media go out of their way to show this kind of harmonious mixing at the religious level. I never see it anyway.

After World War II and the Korean War, many Filipino and Korean immigrants came to the states to become citizens. Following the Vietnam War, many Vietnamese migrated here, as well as some Mong tribesmen who had been loyal to the Americans during the war. Most of these migrants seem to have turned out to be good, loyal American citizens, except for having some language problems. The language issue concerns Mexicans as well, many of whom have become legitimate, satisfied American citizens. California is currently ignoring the language issue as a problem, hoping it will go away, I guess.

It's my opinion that the United States has been terribly weak on foresight since it hasn't properly pursued the language training issue at the time the immigrants became citizens. This has led to enormous expense here in California where the democrat legislature made it a law that all official paperwork be printed in at least six languages. For the state's apparatus to function *economically* such a law should be rescinded and English made the legal language. It's doubtful if this issue being made a law would leave anyone behind; it's a given that help would be available. Resolving the language issue would surely solve a huge number of problems, particularly for California.

While on the subject of language and communication skills, I would opine that we are basically a nation of sensation seekers and we'd be better off spending our spare-time *learning* rather than *being entertained*. For instance, one of the most valuable things one can do with one's time is getting comfortable with the English language. One should, for example, take an unusual word, learn its meaning, and then become able to use it in a sentence.

Whatever it is that one is feeling and would like to be better able to *express*, the English language always has a word for it. One of the most valuable things that one can build in one's personal skill bank is a *large vocabulary*. I suggest that one always have a *thesaurus* and *dic-*

tionary at one's elbow. I sometimes use my two books dozens of times a day. They serve my purposes perfectly because I don't articulate my thoughts well orally, but am better able to articulate them on paper.

GOD AND AMERICA

There are a lot of things about America today that I'm fed up with, but I tell myself that it's the only precious gem left in the universe and is worth fighting for to keep from being destroyed by careless fools. There are huge numbers of bad people in American society, but there are many good people as well. It behooves us Americans who love our country to move closer to our nation's roots, to the learning of what went into the making of our Constitution and, what's more, appreciating it. More than that, we should also move closer to God. After all, He was most important to our nation's founders. Shouldn't we recognize his importance to the nation again?

I surrendered my life to Christ when I was twelve years old. My father, who was a railroad man was not a particularly religious man, but this one evening, he asked me to come along with him to attend a revival meeting to see and hear the phenomenal Aimee Semple MacPherson, who was on a nationwide revival tour.

Maybe it was his curiosity that we went, I don't know. It was a moving evening, and at the end of the service, there was an altar call. Dad and I went forward, and I gave my heart to Christ. *Words cannot describe the elation that I came away with from the service that night.*

I regret to say that in later years I backslid, and it wasn't until after being reunited with my first-love twenty years ago that I also reunited with God. I truly regret that it took me so long to come back to Christ from backsliding, but now I am blessed. I am even learning how to pray. I think that if I were younger, I might have been a good minister, at least from the way I've felt about God in recent years. There is a lot I'd like to have the right opportunity to speak-out about.

Its my observation that there are many people who are troubled, that would give anything just to have the peace of mind that comes with giving one's heart to Christ, but they have to be convinced to give God a try, and that's quite often a big river to cross. It's an absolute thrill, though, to witness the difference in people who surrender themselves to Christ.

I am as critical perhaps of churchgoers as I am of liberals. I'm afraid that there are many hypocritical Christians who talk the talk and walk the walk but who aren't really in touch with God. The few I'm thinking of lack the warmth of sincerity. Even some television pastors come across as seeming charlatans.

(An exceptional Christian man that I must mention is Dr. Charles Stanley, a Baptist minister preaching and televising from Atlanta, Georgia, whom we watch each Sunday morning without fail. He is truly a godly man and one who preaches from the Bible.)

When I reflect on the huge number of troubled liberals in our society, I'm sad that Christianity, the Holy Bible and the Ten Commandments are missing from their daily lives. Bringing the matter up to them, however, often provokes the same tired, old diatribe about the need for division of church and state, an argument that soon falls apart when confronted.

It's come with age in my case, but I'm proud to be able to say that I see the Holy Bible as an unabridged textbook on how to live life. One would think that more people might be disposed to show an interest to learn about God, the Bible, and the Ten Commandments, if for no other reason than to marvel at their enduring nature. Perhaps they're backed off by the millions and millions of outspoken, simple-minded liberals who are offended if the subject is even brought up. It speaks to ignorance, bias, prejudice, etc., when millions of people can pass up a good tip that'd really enrich their lives, yet a tip on a horse race might cause one to be trampled in the rush.

It's my sincere wish that the Christian community might produce a youngish, strong, godly man or woman evangelist, the caliber of Billy Graham, Aimee Semple MacPherson, or Billie Sunday who'd preach from the Bible, who would once again take the message of Jesus

Christ on the road coast-to-coast, celebrating a revival of Christianity.

I make this wish, not just for promoting Christianity, but for the good of the country and, actually, for the sake of the world. It is a time in the nation's history when a deeply Christian evangelist(s) is needed to go into America's cities and the hinterlands to rescue the multitudes of souls desperate for redemption like never before. The nation is truly ripe for it, particularly now, considering how far the country has slipped and with a dangerous radical liberal/progressive administration occupying the White House. Has the nation such an individual?